DATING DETOX

DATING DETOX

40 Days of Perfecting Love
in an
Imperfect World

by
Lisa and Kevin Cotter

Foreword by
Jason and Crystalina Evert

Ignatius Press   Augustine Institute
San Francisco   Greenwood Village, CO

Ignatius Press Distribution
P.O. Box 1339
Fort Collins, CO 80522
Tel: (800) 651-1531
www.ignatius.com

Augustine Institute
6160 S. Syracuse Way, Suite 310
Greenwood Village, CO 80111
Tel: (866) 767-3155
www.augustineinstitute.org

Cover Design: Enrique J. Aguilar Pinto

© 2016 by Ignatius Press, San Francisco,
and the Augustine Institute, Greenwood Village, CO
All rights reserved.
ISBN: 978-0-99720-379-0
Library of Congress Control Number 2016955365

Printed in Canada

Dedication

To the missionaries of FOCUS:
You inspire us more than you will ever know.

CONTENTS

Foreword

In a recent survey of college students, both men and women had nearly double the number of hookups compared to first dates.[1] How many reported feeling desirable or wanted after the hookup? A grand total of two percent.[2] In fact, about seventy percent of college students admitted that they would rather have a traditional romantic relationship than an uncommitted sexual one.[3]

One young woman summed up her discontent by noting, "There is no dating. There's no relationships. ... They're rare. You can have a fling that could last like seven, eight months and you could never actually call someone your 'boyfriend.' [Hooking up] is a lot easier. No one gets hurt—well, not on the surface."[4]

What's going on?

Why is there such a disconnect between what we want and what we settle for?

If we want love, why do we often settle for less?

Over the last twenty years, we have had the blessing to speak on the topics of dating and chastity to young adults across the globe. After every presentation—whether in Australia, England, South Africa, or the Philippines—the students always ask us one thing: "I want to live this message, but what should I do now? How do I stay strong?"

As you know, it's useless to know your destination if you don't know which route to take. Having a goal in mind is noble, but if you don't know how to achieve it, it will remain only a sentimental hope. The same is true when it comes to authentic human love. We need a map, a guide, a blueprint. Otherwise, it's easy to feel discouraged, intimidated, and lost.

If you've ever heard a great talk or read a great book on purity and love, but within a few months (or hours) felt that the ideals seem unattainable, then this book is for you. Whether you hear wedding bells in your near future or you wonder in frustration when the right person will enter your life, the advice in here will prove to be a useful manual for developing your capacity to love. Kevin and Lisa offer a wealth of practical strategies through their own experiences and the raw and honest testimonies of other young adults. The beauty of these stories is that they show how God's plan for our lives (and our love lives) is not ruined even though we often make an impressive mess out of it! To one extent or another, we've all been poisoned by the culture's false ideas of love, dating, and sexuality. No one is unscathed, and we could all use a good detox.

"True love" isn't about finding the perfect person but about weeding out our own imperfections so that we can be free to love. If you are willing to dedicate yourself to this process, then you're actively engaged in marriage preparation—even if you haven't met your future spouse yet! In fact, marriage preparation that begins with the engagement is not true marriage preparation; it's triage. To build a love that lasts, a solid foundation needs to be established now. If you're not sure where to begin, just turn the page and keep on turning for the next forty days. In the meantime, know that we (and the authors of this book) have already been praying for you.

God bless you,
Jason and Crystalina Evert

Introduction

Kathryn was nervous. If you were in her position, you'd probably be nervous, too. On that blistering hot day in central Florida, she had come to a dorm lounge to share her story with me (Lisa). As I looked at the beautiful, blond-haired, blue-eyed sorority girl sitting across from me, I couldn't help but feel a bit nervous myself. I knew what she had come to share with me was deeply personal and might not be easy to tell.

These daily meetings had become a part of my routine as my husband, Kevin, and I began our adventure of writing a book together. Before we put pen to paper, we first desired to spend time listening—listening to the stories of brave souls like Kathryn.

Kathryn began by taking me back to her sophomore year, when she started dating Austin. At first everything was perfect. Having a boyfriend made her feel great, as if she mattered to somebody. Things couldn't have been better.

However, as their relationship began to get physical, Kathryn started to feel uncomfortable. From a young age she had wanted to save sex for marriage, but this was a decision that Austin did not understand. In a campaign to persuade Kathryn to change her mind, he began to challenge her to give him concrete reasons why they shouldn't do it. Despite her best explanations, she could never come up with anything that convinced Austin.

1

Dos and Don'ts

Over Christmas break, Kathryn attended a Catholic young adult conference that a friend had invited her to. While there, she went to a talk on the dos and don'ts of dating. As she listened, excitement started to mount up in her as she finally found the answers she was sure Austin had been looking for. Returning home with copious notes and great enthusiasm, she could hardly wait to share everything with her boyfriend. However, as she relayed each reason for saving sex for marriage, her heart sank further and further as Austin just rolled his eyes and told her that everything she was saying was stupid and invalid.

Kathryn told me, "I felt very inferior to him. He made me believe it was all a silly notion, and two weeks later things went back to how they were before the conference."

Now that Kathryn had abandoned her talk of saving sex, Austin felt triumphant and continued to pressure her to sleep with him. By Valentine's Day, his victory was achieved as worn-out Kathryn finally gave up and lost her virginity to him.

Right Back to Normal

I, too, was at the conference Kathryn attended. In fact, I was in the audience for the dos-and-don'ts-of-dating talk. Although we didn't meet each other until a few years later, I *knew* Kathryn because I had heard her story from both men and women several times before.

In my senior year of high school, I had taken a job as a junior-high youth minister. A few months later, I began working with Kevin as a camp counselor at a Catholic summer camp. Over a decade has passed since then, and we are still doing outreach side by side as a missionary family with FOCUS (the Fellowship of Catholic University Students).

Our life as missionaries has afforded us the opportunity to travel the country speaking to and investing in youth and young adults in very personal ways. We've listened to stories, heard of struggles and triumphs, and advised in whatever ways we can.

At many a conference, congress, retreat, mission trip, or talk, the spark for leading a pure life was ignited in a person's heart. The truth that following God's plans for love, dating, and sex would lead to happiness finally clicked. It wasn't just about rules—it was about being truly free to love and be loved, and they knew they wanted it—but. ... But, a few weeks later the high was gone and everything went right back to normal.

Losing the High

Six weeks after speaking at a conference for ten thousand college students last year, my heart was heavy for the men and women like Kathryn in attendance. I knew where they were at.

There were men who had finally gotten up enough courage to take their sins to Confession. But now they were right back where they started. They wondered, "What's wrong with me? Why can't I control myself?"

There were women who were done defining their value by whether or not a guy flirted with them. But they were back to trying to hide the fact that they felt worthless. "So what if nobody shows interest. Why do I need a man to make me feel beautiful anyway?" they'd ask in frustration.

The pleasures of the world were pulling and they were struggling to fight back. With their heads hung in defeat, they'd reluctantly gone back to the superficial fixes that masked their pain and satisfied their desires for the moment. They *knew* they didn't want the world's way of love, dating, and sex anymore, and they *knew* that following God's vision was the answer ... but how? How were they supposed to get from wanting it to actually living it?

In that moment an idea came to me: *Someone should write a book on how to do just that—a book on how to move from wanting it to living it.*

The Journey

What you are holding in your hands is the result of that thought. It's a book for those who are tired of the empty promises of our culture's plan for love, dating, and sex. It's for those who are worn out from giving away their hearts and bodies only to have them returned bruised and broken. It's for anyone who after a hookup or breakup has thought, "That wasn't right, that's not what I really wanted—*There must be something more.*"

There *is* more. But getting to that "more" requires a willingness to take a journey—a journey from where you are to where you hope to be.

Some of you may already be on this journey. Others of you may be staring at the path wondering whether you should take the first step. Wherever you are, when you picked up this book you picked up a guide that was created to show you the way. If you are ready to take your first, or next, step toward living the freedom of God's plan for love, dating, and sex, then this book is for you.

Before You Begin

You'll notice that the book is divided into forty bite-size chapters. To get the most out of this experience, we recommend you read one chapter a day over a forty-day period. By reading the book in this way, our hope is that you will be able to process its contents bit by bit and immediately begin to apply it to your life. If you do miss a day (or three) just pick back up and start where you left off.

At the end of each week, there are study questions on that week's theme. Whether you are reading the book in a group setting, with a friend, or on your own, we encourage you to make use of the questions.

Finally, to make the book come alive, we've spent dozens of hours interviewing young adults. All the stories found within these pages are true, although the names of all individuals have been changed to preserve their privacy. As you will see, the brave souls who shared their stories with us have made mistakes and have wounds that they carry with them, but they have not let their past hinder them from moving beyond what they've done—or what's been done to them. You'll see from their stories that anyone, truly anyone, can take this journey toward authentically living God's plan for love, dating, and sex.

WEEK 1: GETTING STARTED

Welcome to the first week of your detox. Take a deep breath. It's time to begin.

Day 1: The Summit

Fifty-three. That's the official number of peaks in Colorado that exceed fourteen thousand feet in elevation. As Coloradans, we simply call them fourteeners. Scaling a fourteener is not for the timid. Thin air, rough terrain, unpredictable weather—it's no walk in the park.

When you stand at the base of a fourteener, the summit you are aiming for isn't always visible. First, it may well be dark—if you want to make it to the top in one day, you sometimes have to set out in the dark before the sun even rises. Second, even if you can wait to begin your ascent in the light, it is still rare to see your desired peak, as other terrain often obscures it.

So to begin a journey to the top of a fourteener you have to set out in faith: faith that there is a path that will actually get you where you want to go, faith that if you stick to it, then you'll reach the peak you can't see.

If you don't despair at the magnitude of your goal and give up before taking your first step, an ascent begins with only one sure thing: the journey will be unpredictable. There will be times when you round a bend thinking a much-needed flat stretch will meet you, but instead you find a rock-filled incline. What starts as a calm, sunny day may become a windy mess and you will wish you had remembered your parka. Your lungs may fail you, and your lack of fear of heights will suddenly become a thing of the past. As we said, it's unpredictable.

But if you can persevere through the challenges, bright spots will surprise you. Random downhill patches filled with wildflowers will come out of nowhere. When you start feeling isolated, interesting mountain creatures will greet you. (We're not just talking about fellow hikers, although hiking with them for a stint can be a lot of fun.)

And then there's the summit. After miles and miles of journeying, there you are, standing on top of the world. Breathtaking views surround you, and the feeling of accomplishment is unsurpassable. You tested your physical and mental limits and came out victorious.

One Step Each Day

Holding this book may feel like standing at the base of a fourteener. You know this forty-day journey is going to be a lot of work, and you probably want to take it, but maybe you doubt that living God's vision for love, dating, and sex is even possible. Like the summit of a fourteener, you can't see it, which makes you wonder whether you can get there—or whether it even exists.

We hear you, and believe us, we've been there, too: failed relationships that end with a dramatic flair, botched attempts to live the way you know you want to live, guilt and shame about the past mixed with fear about the future. When you add it all together, making peace with love, dating, and sex in our crazy world can seem like an impossible challenge. *But that's where this book comes in.* Forty days of purifying yourself from the junk you've been fed by our imperfect world. Forty days of intentionally building new habits and skills needed to make authentic love possible. Forty days of reordering your view of love, dating, and sex so you can be free to love and be loved—because *you were made to love and be loved.*

Will you step out in faith? Will you believe that there is a way to get where you want to go and that if you stick to it you'll reach your destination? Yes, the journey will be unpredictable. It will have ups and downs, triumphs and struggles, joys and sorrows. There will be times when you will doubt whether you can make it and you'll want to give up. You will face setbacks that will feel insurmountable. Your limits will be tested and you will face fears you didn't even know you had. But don't panic. You can do this. This book was designed to help you to do this.

All you have to do to complete this process is take one step each day. Don't worry about the step you need to take tomorrow, next week, or next month; just make a commitment for today. Then tomorrow do the same, and the day after that, do the same. If you happen to fall down along the way, just get back up and keep going, one step a day, until you reach the top. And when you arrive at the summit, you can stand there and soak in the breathtaking view knowing that you pushed yourself to the limit and did what you set out to do. Trust us, the payoff will be worth every step.

The Detox

The purpose of a detox is to remove some type of toxic substance from a person's life. If someone wishes to be free of toxins caused by a drug or alcohol addiction, then he or she goes through a period of detoxification as the body works to repair long-term damage. If someone wishes to remove food related toxins, then that person might try a diet detox by eliminating bad foods and incorporating good foods in an effort to restore overall health. And for people who want to remove the toxic influences that are leaving them disillusioned by love, we suggest they go on a *dating* detox.

Our lives are filled with toxins that are destroying our ability to love and be loved. Some of these toxins are caused by our own mistakes, and some are influenced by our imperfect world's tainted view of love, dating, and sex. Like it or not, no matter who we are, we have all been affected.

In order to purify ourselves of these influences we not only need to remove unhealthy habits that are poisoning our lives, but we also need to reorder our understanding of love, dating, and sex, and build good habits that will restore our ability to love. This is where the daily detox challenge comes in.

Each day when you pick up this book you'll be given something new to consider about life, love, dating, sex, and relationships. At the end of the chapter you will be presented with a concrete detox challenge. Some days you will be invited to remove something from your life. Some days you will be asked to add something in. And some days you will be asked to reconsider your understanding of a concept. The purpose of these challenges is to help you detox from the poisonous influences in your life and bring you to a place of freedom so you can love and be loved.

When we change our actions we can change our lives, so if you want to get the most out of this book, we invite you to take these detox challenges seriously. Fear not—most of them are quick and easy, some of them are even fun, and all of them have a purpose. So reap the benefits and make them happen!

Today's Detox Challenge

One of the greatest challenges to finishing this book may be forgetting to read it. So right now we suggest you set an alarm or make a calendar appointment for when you will read this book tomorrow—and for the following thirty-eight days after that. When the reminder goes off, either drop what you are doing and read, or set another reminder for when you will do it later.

One more thing: Several of the daily challenges include writing things down, so it might be helpful for you to find a place to keep your lists and thoughts. Grab a new journal, tear out the used pages of an old notebook, or create a document on your computer or a note on your phone. However you roll, we suggest you put it all down in one place and keep it close to the book. From here on out, when we mention your journal, what we are referring to is the unique place you have set aside for note-taking.

Day 2: Accountability

Leo was the kind of guy any mom would want her daughter to date. In high school, he played football, basketball, and ran track. He sang in the choir and starred in musicals. He went to Mass on Sunday. He was faithful to his girlfriend, and when he felt a potential call to the priesthood, they broke up for a stint so that he could consider it further. From the outside, everything was perfect, but if you dug a bit deeper, Leo wasn't being completely forthright.

During Leo's two-year relationship with his high school sweetheart, they refrained from having sex, but were physically intimate in other ways. After the relationship ended, Leo realized he had become accustomed to having his physical, emotional, and social desires met, and he soon missed it. Despite his lingering thoughts of the priesthood, he began hopping from girl to girl, trying to get the high back.

"It got even worse during my first year of college," Leo explained. "I let loose, and that was when I would hook up with multiple girls on a weekend. I was not in a good place ... I remember telling these girls I cared about them just because I wanted to have physical pleasure." Leo had resorted to using women physically, and he knew it.

Later that fall, when a group of seminarians came to visit his campus, Leo was blindsided by their presence. They reminded him of a call to greatness that he was running from.

Leo thought, "What have I been doing with my life? For the past three months I've been slapping [Jesus] in the face. How long will I put off this holiness thing so I can keep seeking pleasure?"

That day, Leo went to the campus parish and sought out a priest to talk to. Inspired again, he tried to turn a new leaf, but it wasn't long before he was disappointed to find himself hooking

13

up at a party ... again. In that moment, Leo knew that if he was going to succeed in controlling his habit of seeking out physical highs, he needed some consistent help because despite his best efforts, he kept falling back into his same old ways.

Josh's Support

It was around this time that Leo met Josh. Josh and Leo had very similar personalities and they immediately clicked. There was something different about Josh that struck Leo. In Josh, Leo saw the peace that he desired but had failed to obtain. Recognizing this, Leo began to share his struggles with Josh, who was quick to offer his support.

Leo explained, "I started hanging out with Josh whenever I could. I just needed to be in his presence because what he was doing every day was for Christ." This was exactly how Leo wanted to live his life.

With Leo's permission, Josh began to keep Leo accountable for his desire to live a truly pure life. Because Leo had shared that he struggled with hooking up at parties, Josh would check in with him on weekends and invite him to come hang out with his friends instead. When Leo battled with objectifying women, Josh was there as a sounding board to help him sort through what to do. Josh became Leo's "go-to" guy whenever he was struggling.

With the support of Josh and the accountability he asked of Leo, Leo has finally been able to succeed in consistently living the life he desires to live.

Accountability

When setting out to pursue a big or difficult goal, it's not abnormal to seek the support of others and to make yourself accountable to them. Gyms have personal trainers, universities have advisors, and businesses have mentors, because it works to have a particular person whose job is to push others to achieve their goal.

One of the key pieces of Leo's continual success in leading a chaste life was having Josh around to keep him accountable for his actions. Leo welcomed Josh's inquiries into how things were going because he knew he needed the support of a friend to help him move beyond his struggles. Hooking up was not leading to his happiness. He wanted to be free of falling back into the old habits that left him disappointed in himself and feeling like he was slapping Jesus in the face. Knowing that Josh was going to ask if he had slipped up recently made it easier for Leo to say no to his desires to use someone physically; being able to give a good report about himself motivated him.

To wrap things up, Leo added, "I still struggle every day. The battle against sin never ends. Only a fool would think he would stop being tempted. Yet the tide has turned in my favor significantly. Having Josh as a close friend and brother in Christ challenges me to be a better man and Christian."

Ultimately Josh points Leo back to Jesus. He helps him to stand firm in his convictions and get outside his own head so he can see things clearly, which is just the kind of support Leo needed to succeed.

Today's Detox Challenge

We bet you can predict what today's challenge will be. Yep, you got it—today we invite you to ask someone to be your accountability partner. Your partner's job will be twofold.

First, we hope this person can help make sure you finish this book. To add a little incentive to the mix, we suggest you give your accountability partner thirty-eight dollars. No, you are not paying your partner to keep you accountable. The thirty-eight dollars is meant to be given back to you, one dollar for each chapter you read. If you finish this book, you'll get all your money back, but if you decide not to finish it, your accountability partner will keep a dollar for each chapter you didn't read.

Second, we hope your partner will ask you how the journey is going. You might even consider meeting weekly to discuss your progress and talk over the discussion questions at the end of each week.

Right now, we want you to think about whom you can ask to keep you accountable. It could be a friend, family member, mentor, youth minister, or Bible study leader ... really anybody you trust to give it to you straight and not shy away from pushing you to succeed. Once you have your person in mind, we suggest you send a text right away. Let him or her know you have a favor to ask and would love to get together ASAP.

Day 3: You Can't Do This

When Elizabeth headed off to college, she dove right in to the clichéd college experience of partying and hooking up. Yet, right before the beginning of her second semester, she somehow found herself at a Catholic conference for university students. There the message of leading a pure life pierced her heart, and she deeply desired to make some changes in her approach to dating and relationships. Her enthusiasm was so high that at the conference she actually bought herself a chastity ring to remind her of the day she started over. Shortly after the conference, however, everything went right back to normal, and the partying and hooking up resumed.

Over the next few years, Elizabeth continued to struggle with how she wanted to live versus how she was actually living.

"I started to doubt if that experience at the conference was even real," she explained. "I had God on one side, but my heart wasn't there. I didn't know how to fix the divide between my intellectual knowledge and my lifestyle."

In a painful turn of events, Elizabeth was taken advantage of at a party while she was blacked out from drinking too much. She was so heartbroken that she all but gave up on what now seemed like a distant ideal—that of living the freedom she knew following God's plans for love, dating, and sex would offer her.

"After that I was numb to the effects of being sexually active," recalled Elizabeth. "I started to regularly hook up with a guy and it just didn't bother me anymore ... and I didn't even feel bad about it, which annoyed me."

"I Don't Like Chastity!"

Even though Elizabeth had almost given up on God and his plans, God had not given up on Elizabeth. One night, still restless over her torn lifestyle, she couldn't take it anymore. In a moment of desperation, she called out to God with what she described as the most honest prayer she had ever prayed.

"I don't like chastity!" Elizabeth yelled at God. "Why don't you give me the desire for it? *I want to want it!*" she begged. "And then the strength I needed hit me like an arrow. I was keenly aware of God's presence. I had finally been honest with him and *actually* prayed about it for the first time."

Before that night, Elizabeth hadn't really been truthful about her struggles with leading a sexually pure life and her need for God's strength to make any real changes. After that intense moment, she tried to be honest with God as she worked to develop a genuine relationship with him. She began to notice that when she was consistently spending time talking to God in prayer, she was able to live a pure life, but if she let that time slide, things would start to fall apart again.

"There was a time over Christmas break when I got out of my routine and didn't pray for a month or two. When I returned to school I hit a huge road bump and hooked up with the guy I used to hook up with. After that experience, I *knew* that God's strength was the only thing that was going to help me be chaste. It solidified the truth that prayer is necessary."

As we finished our conversation, Elizabeth shared with us that since she got back into her prayer routine, she hasn't had a major fall. "It's not always easy," she said, "but at least now I know that you can't do it alone. It's his strength that helps us to keep moving forward."

You Can't Do This Alone

As you embark on this journey, there is one thing you need to know. As Elizabeth learned, you can't do this alone. Without God in the picture, you will not finish this book, and living according to God's designs will be an unbearable struggle. Detoxing from the world's imperfect view of love, dating, and sex, figuring out how to succeed in following God's plans, moving beyond your past ... none of these things are easy. But if you can truly invite God into the equation, anything is possible.

If, like Elizabeth, you want to make real changes in your life, the first step is to invite God into the process and start praying every day. Now, before you despair without even giving it a try, know that *prayer doesn't have to be complicated or elaborate*. All you have to do is talk to God like you would talk to a friend. Be real with him. Tell him your thoughts, doubts, and fears. Tell him what's bothering you and what's making you come alive. Tell him what you need and thank him for what he's done. Even though he already knows all these things, he still wants to hear it from *you*—just like you still want to hear a friend's big news in person, even if you already know via social media.

Awkward

Learning to talk to God like a friend can be awkward at first, but just because it's awkward doesn't mean it's not worth it. As in any relationship, it takes time for people to get to a place where they feel comfortable. So, to make this process less strange, most people find it helpful to come up with a plan for what they will do when they take the time to pray. A simple plan might go something like this:

- Close your eyes, take a few deep breaths, and clear your mind.

- Read a passage from the Bible or from a daily devotional book.[1]

- Consider how the reading applies to your life, and ask God if he has anything for you to think over in light of what you read.

- Without holding anything back, talk to God about how you are doing, let him know what you and others need, and finally, thank him for the ways he has blessed you.

Prayer is one of those things that takes time to get comfortable with, but as you saw with Elizabeth, and as we heard over and over again in our interviews, it's a necessary part of learning how to love and be loved. Remember, you can't do this on your own, but if you invite God into the picture, anything is possible.

Today's Detox Challenge

We hope you already have a reminder for when you are going to read each day. From here on out, when the reminder goes off we challenge you to spend some time having a conversation with God before you begin to read.

If you are new to prayer, we encourage you to spend a few minutes right now coming up with a plan for what you will do during your daily time with God. Aim for five minutes in the beginning, and once you get consistent with that, add on five more, then five more, and so on until you reach at least twenty minutes every day. If, by the end of this book, you are still working on getting in five minutes, don't stress about it. The most important thing is to show up. God will be there, and he will be delighted to hear from you.

Day 4: Damaged Goods

Have you ever heard analogies about the ways in which impure actions can leave an irreversible mark on a person? The empty tube of toothpaste that will never be free of crinkles again, even if you try to shove the paste back in? Or the crumpled-up piece of paper that will never be smooth again, no matter how hard you try to flatten it back out? Their messages are clear: you can never go back if you screw up purity—so don't blow it because if you do, then you're damaged goods.

The Poster Child

At fourteen, Brad lost his virginity to a girl he "didn't really know or find attractive." The experience wasn't all that he had hoped it would be, so shortly after that, he tried a different approach to sexual intimacy and entered into an exclusive relationship. When that ended with his girlfriend cheating on him, Brad decided that sex and relationships were just complicated, so he began to pursue women only for whatever temporary pleasure he could get from them.

Perhaps unfortunately for Brad, his natural charm and likability made hooking up with girls entirely too easy. His weekends were spent partying and prowling around for the next girl he could manipulate into being used for physical pleasure. When he went on vacation, he would use a fake name and fill his time looking for a random girl to have a fling with.

Shaking his head, Brad admitted, "I physically used women and I was good at it. I liked the emotional affirmation and the pleasures that came with it. It made me feel not so average. Flirting and hooking up made me feel popular and powerful." In sum, Brad was the poster child for the player to avoid.

Despite his wayward life, God still desired to call Brad to something better, so he continued to knock patiently on his heart. Slowly Brad began to respond by giving God little pieces at a time, but he hesitantly held on to his habit of hooking up.

Fed Up

During Christmas break of his sophomore year of college, Brad attended a five-day event devoted to teaching college students how to bring Jesus to their campuses. After hearing talks on prayer, virtue, and discipleship, Brad found himself somewhat reluctantly making out with a random conference attendee. Things continued to escalate but they stopped just short of sleeping together. As soon as it was over, Brad could hardly believe what he had just done.

That night, he finally became fed up with his polarizing lifestyle and, in a moment of grace, fully let God in. While kneeling in adoration, he begged the Lord to help him truly give his life to Christ and curb his pleasure-seeking use of women.

Determined to succeed, he began to work incredibly hard to form new habits that didn't include chasing after his next hookup. Slowly it became easier and easier, but as a guy who had already "crumpled up his piece of paper" over and over again, he worried that any real chance to start anew might already be lost. He had a sinking feeling in his stomach as he wondered if once a girl found out who he used to be, she might not be able to love him—mistakes, baggage, and all.

You Are Not a Lost Cause

Despite the well-meaning people who use analogies of empty toothpaste tubes and crumpled paper for the harm done by impurity, these comparisons can leave people like Brad with little or no hope. After being told that irreversible damage has been done, wanting a chance to start over seems like a joke.

Perhaps this is you. Perhaps, like Brad, you've come to believe that hitting reset is impossible. If so, we are so sorry if no one has told you this before, but that is a lie from Hell. No matter what you've done or how many times you've done it, God will never see you as a lost cause or a screw up that no one could actually *love*. Get that out of your head right now, because there are few surer ways to stop you from finishing this book. It's never too late. No matter how far you think you've gone, forgiveness and restoration are always possible.

Let It Go

One of the first steps Brad took in beginning anew was going to Jesus in the Sacrament of Reconciliation and acknowledging his past sins of ignoring God's plan for sexual intimacy. In Confession, he found the strength he needed to move forward, as he felt God's grace, forgiveness, and mercy pour over him. As Brad wrestled with the idea that his past might make it impossible for him to deserve authentic love, he brought his self-pity and worry to Confession as well. Over time, he began to believe that he was forgiven, and this knowledge gave him hope, because if God could love him and forgive him, then perhaps others could do the same.

Accepted

We hope you're not surprised to hear that Brad was right. Others *have* been able to look beyond his past and love him despite his mistakes. As he described it, God blessed him with "people who loved me through it and didn't let my past bother them because they knew that God was working in my life."

God wants to work in your life, too. He wants to forgive you through the Sacrament of Reconciliation. He wants to bless you with people who will love you and accept you—mistakes, baggage, and all.

Today's Detox Challenge

Over the next few weeks we challenge you to carve out some time to seek out Jesus's love, mercy, and forgiveness in Confession. We know that going can be tough, but the graces flowing from the sacrament put God back in charge and weaken the power of guilt, shame, and confusion that can consume your battle.

Whether you just went last week or haven't been since your First Confession, it doesn't matter. Jesus will be waiting there with open arms, ready to give you the strength you need to believe that you can begin anew.

If you don't know what time your parish offers Confession, we invite you to go online right now and look it up. If you're afraid that going to your parish priest will be awkward, then look up the next closest parish and plan to go there. If all else fails, call a parish and set up an appointment.

Day 5: Triggers

In order to succeed on this journey, your actions need to start reflecting God's plans for love, dating, and sex. Throughout these weeks we will be diving into what exactly that is, but for now, we want you to lay some ground rules for yourself based upon what you already know about living according to God's plan.

Although we won't normally invite you to use your journal at the beginning of a chapter, we recommend that you get it out right now and write down a list of sexually related behaviors that you know are not in line with God's design for love. Go ahead, put down your book and start writing.

Now that you have hopefully finished your list, we are going to recommend that you commit to avoiding the acts you listed for the time being. Later in this book we will address *why* they will not lead to your happiness, but until then, just don't do them ... and good luck!

Just kidding—we've got a plan to help you with this challenge, but first we have a story to share.

That Cecilia

Cecilia was raised in a Christian home where she was taught to love Jesus—and she did. However, despite being active in her Christian Faith, Cecilia and her boyfriend slowly took the physical side of their relationship one step further after each breakup and reconciliation. Eventually, all that was left was sleeping together. Once that was done, when they broke up the next time, it was for good.

At this time, Cecilia left for college and started making new relationships with guys. Attributing it to the fact that she had already lost her virginity, Cecilia explained to us that messing around with guys became a lot easier and, despite not really wanting to do it, she began to make a habit out of it.

She recalled, "I'd go over to these guys' houses and I'd think, 'I'm being a good Christian influence on them, nothing will happen when I go over there,' but it always did. I eventually had to admit that I didn't have control over myself. When the emotions turned on I was a completely different person and I knew I couldn't allow *that* Cecilia to come around because she couldn't be trusted."

Eventually Cecilia was able to be real with herself and acknowledge that if she went to a guy's house, then, despite her good intentions, something *would* happen. So what did she do? She stopped going.

Triggers

Your brain is designed to remember patterns. This is why every day when you wake up you don't have to relearn how to speak, walk, read, or write. When the brain starts to notice patterns, it assumes that you are repeating an action because you want to get good at it and make a habit out of it.

Think about when you get in a car. You hardly have to think about putting a seat belt on because your brain says, "Oh, I'm sitting in a car, I know what to do—grab the seat belt."

The same goes with any pattern. When you put your shoes on, you tie them; when you smell dinner, you want to eat it; when you jump into the deep end of a pool, you swim. Certain actions, environments, and sequences work as triggers in your life that lead you to react in habitual ways.

For this reason, it can be more important to pay attention to what happens right *before* you do something than what happens when you are actually doing it, especially if it's an action that you know you'll later regret.

Identifying Your Triggers

We asked several of the interviewees to identify triggers that set them up to deviate from God's plan for love, dating, and sex. We've listed the most common ones below.

Alcohol or drugs: When your mind is impaired it can be difficult to make good decisions. Even a slight buzz can weaken your judgment and lead you to do things that you wouldn't do if you were in full control of yourself. As one interviewee put it, "Drugs and alcohol would always numb my conscience and consequently my morality."

Darkness: Getting caught up in the moment is significantly easier to do in the dark. Darkness hides things, but if your interactions are kept in the light, you'll be able to see more clearly, both physically and mentally.

Closed doors: Although this isn't always possible, it's helpful to allow yourself to be interrupted. Something as simple as leaving a door open or hanging out in a common space ensures that you don't do anything you wouldn't want your grandma to see you doing.

Lying down together: If you want to ensure that you don't find yourself in a difficult situation with another person, keep two feet on the floor. We know it sounds extreme, but if you're serious about avoiding sexual regrets, the "keep your feet on the floor" rule helps.

Screen binging: For many people, their chill-time default involves glaring at a screen. When you do this alone, or even with someone else, it can lead to loneliness and boredom. Both of these feelings can trigger a whole host of problems. Monitor your screen time and if you notice that you're getting lonely or bored, get up and get out before one thing leads to another.

In addition to these general triggers, everybody has specific triggers that are unique to them. A particular person, location, social media site, app, book, type of music, or even smell (pot or alcohol anyone?) can lead you to engage in regrettable actions.

So think back: What happens before you cross the line sexually? Do you get dressed up, go out, and start drinking? Do you head over to someone's house and watch a movie in a dark room? Do you watch porn followed by texting with your ex? What situations, moods, environments, or actions lead you to the point of no return?

Knowing and understanding your personal triggers can help you avoid them, which will in turn give you a better chance of avoiding the regrets that come after.

Today's Detox Challenge

What are your triggers? Today we propose that you call them out for what they are and write them down on a fresh page in your journal. Then, for the next twenty-four hours, we invite you to commit to avoiding these triggers or setting parameters for them, such as giving yourself a curfew if late nights are a trigger for you. Twenty-four hours—that's it. We're just suggesting that you try it out for one full day.

Day 6: The Fast

In our years with FOCUS, we've seen that missionaries do a lot of crazy things. They fundraise their salaries. They move wherever they are told throughout the country. They talk to strangers about Jesus. But perhaps one of the most shocking things they do is give up dating for an entire year. That's right—all first-year missionaries fast from romantic relationships for one year.

When you fast from earthly goods, such as giving up meat on Fridays during Lent, you don't do it because meat is bad or evil. You do it because you want to ensure that you are in control of your body, and that your body is not in control of you.

Coffee

Let's say every morning you have a cup (or three) of coffee to wake you up—until one morning your coffeemaker breaks. So you order a new one online and think, "I can go a few days without caffeine." After three painful mornings of obsessing over your missing cup(s) of coffee, you realize you can't. You vow never again to order anything of importance online and hop in line at the local coffee shop.

In this scenario, were you in control of yourself and free to do what you wanted to do? We say, "Not really." Sure, you were free in the sense that the coffee police didn't barge in on your morning routine and rip the cup out of your hands to inform you that your actions were now illegal; but after three days of headaches, crabbiness, and exhaustion, you realized that you weren't free to say no to coffee without some undesirable side effects. Instead of you being in control of the coffee, the coffee was in control of you.

FOCUS doesn't ask its missionaries to fast from dating because dating in and of itself is bad; rather, FOCUS asks its missionaries to fast from dating because if we are not careful, then having a romantic relationship can turn into an addiction—it can become something we just *have to have*. And if we don't have one, it can become something we obsess about. Sounds a lot like our coffee, huh?

Freedom

If you desire to be free to love and be loved, you cannot be addicted to the idea that being in a relationship equals love. Your happiness cannot depend on whether or not you have a boyfriend or girlfriend, and the best way to understand this is to find happiness without one. This is not to say that true happiness comes from isolation. On the contrary, it comes from loving and being loved by God and others. But if we base our happiness solely on being addicted to the emotional and physical need for a romantic relationship, then our happiness is a false happiness.

The fast from romantic relationships that FOCUS asks its missionaries to undertake is more than just not holding hands or not going on a date. It's a mindset they invite them to have—a mindset of not seeing every person as a potential boyfriend or girlfriend. It's meant to give the missionaries the freedom to *not* obsess about who will next fill their "relationship status" on social media. It allows them to step back and see dating and love through new lenses, so they can reenter the world of relationships with clarity when the fast is over.

Today's Detox Challenge

Over the last twenty-four hours, we challenged you to stay away from your triggers, or to put parameters around them. How did it go? Were you able to do it? If so, how do you feel today? Good?

Hopeful? Proud? We hope so. If you were able to succeed, you have just proven to yourself that it is possible. Yes, you can do it!

If you did not meet the challenge, don't worry. Today is a new day, and we are challenging you again to commit to avoiding or to putting restrictions on your triggers for another twenty-four hours. Ready. Go.

And one more thing: today we suggest you take a break from dating for the duration of this process. (Sorry if you thought you were going to get out of this one, but what would a dating detox be without eliminating dating for a time!) If you want to do this detox right, you're going to need to clear some space to do it. Starting a new relationship while you're in the midst of it can complicate things. Perhaps at no other time in your life will you be given permission to focus primarily on God, love, and where you fit into the picture. So do yourself a favor and allow yourself to engage fully in this journey. It's only for thirty-three more days, which someday will seem like a blip on the radar screen of life.

For those of you who are currently in a relationship, we're not suggesting that you completely break up, but we do think it would be very beneficial for you to set some temporary boundaries for your relationship. This will help give you the space you need to do this detox well. Perhaps cut out texting (radical, we know) or limit the amount of time you spend together. Maybe you can commit to not communicating via social media, or to hanging out only in group settings. Basically we're asking you to consider taking a bit of a retreat within your relationship so you can think clearly about the big picture of relationships, love, and what it all means, without constantly applying your thoughts to just the here and now.

If you are willing to take this step, find some time to discuss these ideas with your boyfriend or girlfriend and figure out what will work best for you as a couple. As you navigate the conversation, remember that the purpose of the fast is not to create distance between you. It is to help you grow as individuals, which will in turn strengthen your relationship and love as a couple. With this in mind, perhaps you can even invite your boyfriend or girlfriend to take this journey with you by reading the book as well.

Day 7: Singleness Is Not a Disease

Whether you're in seventh grade or twenty-seven, you've probably been asked by unwelcome inquirers, "So, do you have a boyfriend/girlfriend?" Grandma, your aunt, your sibling's friend, your dental hygienist—they all want to know. And it seems that no matter how they respond to your reply of "no," you feel as if you have to defend your status so they don't think there's something wrong with you.

The good news is that singleness is actually not a disease. There is nothing wrong with you if you aren't currently attached—in fact, as of yesterday, we're asking you to be *intentionally* unattached for the time being. So you don't need to see a doctor, you don't need to start a treatment program, and you don't need to obsess about it. Now that you are, we hope, on a temporary dating fast (or taking a retreat within your current relationship), we want you to leverage this time.

It's Not My Nightmare

Before Andrea left for college, her faith community sent her off with a challenge to begin her experience with a dating fast. Feeling up for it, she agreed. At first it was smooth sailing as Andrea easily filled her time with the demands of her engineering major and lively community. Before long, however, Jake entered the picture and soon it became clear that he was interested in starting a relationship.

Andrea was torn. Jake seemed like the perfect guy for her, but she had made a commitment to hold off on dating for the time being. She took the matter to prayer and asked God, "If you don't want me to be with him, take him away." The very next day Jake told her that he was going on a trip for a month and when he came back, he told her all about his new girlfriend.

After that experience, Andrea decided to move forward with her fast with confidence and complete abandon, and she was glad she did.

"You can't imagine how much you can grow in your relationship with God when you don't have a guy on your mind." Andrea shared with genuine enthusiasm. "My prayer went very deep because I wasn't thinking about other things. It was like being on a retreat. I was able to put my eyes on what was important and in the moment, and I had the privilege of seeing him be there in moments when I wouldn't have otherwise. I learned to rely on God for everything and if it weren't for my fast, I wouldn't have given myself so completely to him."

Closeness with God was not the only gift Andrea was given as a result of her fast. She also learned to let go of her phobia about being alone.

"I don't have a great fear or anxiety about not finding a guy. It's not my nightmare and it doesn't occupy my whole day. Of course," she added with a smile, "I'd love to have one eventually, but for now I know I'll always find something to do, and I feel like that is a blessing of the fast. Just rest in him and let him be in charge of your love life."

What's the Plan?

God is always working and he always has a plan, but sometimes we can be so focused on our plan that we forget to let him chime in with a few ideas of his own. Maybe he wants you to reach out to someone who needs a friend. Maybe he's been dropping some hints about a project or ministry he wants you to get involved in. Maybe now is the perfect time for you to start working toward that goal on your bucket list that God has left at least four memos about, but you've disregarded them all.

What's in front of you right now? Discovering God's plans can be as simple as this: looking up and looking out at the good things God is surrounding you with, as opposed to looking down and looking in for some good things you *wish* he was surrounding you with. God has a plan for you right now! You have a mission—a life to live—that only *you* can live right now! What are you waiting for?

Today's Detox Challenge

The single life allows a certain level of freedom that those who are married, engaged, or even just dating don't have. Today we challenge you to take advantage of this time of singleness and set a goal that you can accomplish before the end of these forty days. Master the grill, memorize a favorite psalm, serve at a soup kitchen, hike a new trail— whatever is on your bucket list, pick an item that you know you can achieve before your journey is over and get out there and make it happen.

Finally, how did the second day of being conscious of your triggers go? Since you'll likely be so busy coming up with plans for that goal you'll be accomplishing, you probably won't have time to be bored enough to worry about your triggers; but just in case, spend one more day avoiding/putting parameters on them. And congratulations, you've made it through the first week of this book!

Discussion Questions for Week 1

1. What do you think about the detox challenges in
    this book? What do you hope to accomplish by
    participating in them?

2. Throughout Week 1, you heard several stories about
    people hitting their breaking point and knowing
    that their lives needed to change. Have you ever hit a
    breaking point in your life? What inspired you to make
    a change?

3. We shared several tools to help you live a life of au-
    thentic love (for instance, accountability, prayer, and
    going to Confession). How have these been helpful to
    you in the past? How have they been difficult?

4. There is a stark contrast between the world's vision for
    love, dating, and sex, and God's vision. How do you
    handle this contrast in your own life? What do you say
    when people question you about it?

5. What do you think of the idea of temporarily giving
    up dating? What are the first objections that come
    to mind?

6. Why might a dating fast be helpful? Are you planning
    to go on a dating fast?

WEEK 2: MADE FOR LOVE

You spent all last week laying some important foundations for this journey. You've been invited to find an accountability partner, have a conversation with God each day, go to Confession, identify and avoid your triggers, take a break from dating, and set an exciting goal for yourself that will be completed by the end of this process. Step back and think about it: in one week you've made huge strides on this journey.

If you haven't accomplished all of these challenges perfectly, then you're not a failure. Today is the beginning of a new week, so pick yourself up and start again. After all, you are still reading this. Be proud of yourself.

We're excited about what's ahead for you this week as you really get going on this journey. It's great to strive to live the way you want to live for a week, but if you want this to be a sustained way of living, you've got to start thinking about how to make that possible for the long haul.

Day 8: Something More

Last week we asked you to set a goal of accomplishing something that has been sitting on your bucket list. We hope it is a good one and that you've already started taking steps toward achieving it.

Imagine with us that the goal you set was to see the world's most visited museum—the Louvre in Paris. (We know it's a pretty audacious goal, but just work with us on this one.) Boasting 652,300 square feet and nearly 350,000 works of art and artifacts from ancient to modern times, you want nothing more than to take it all in with your own eyes.

After scraping together every nickel and dime you can find, you hop on a flight to Paris. When the plane lands you grab some caffeine to fight off jet lag and navigate your way through the City of Love until you catch your first glimpse of the historic Louvre in the distance. You're pumped as you realize that your moment to see works like the *Venus de Milo* and Leonardo da Vinci's *Mona Lisa* has finally come. With your walking shoes on and guidebook in hand, you are ready to be the first in line when the doors open.

As you approach the glass Louvre Pyramid entrance, you notice officers outside directing people away from the museum. Determined to discover why the museum is closed, you march up to an officer and demand an explanation. However, once the reason has been revealed, you almost wish you hadn't asked.

In the middle of the night a band of vandals snuck into the museum undetected, and in the few moments they had before the authorities arrived, they managed to damage a number of ancient works of art, including the *Venus de Milo* and the *Mona Lisa*, which you were so eager to see. Devastated, you trudge back to your hotel room and check the Internet to see if you can learn more details.

Not surprisingly, social media sites are blowing up with the news. People are passionately commenting on what's being called a tragedy, conspiracy theories are starting to form, and experts are weighing in as everyone tries to figure out the answer to one question: "Why?" Why would someone destroy such beloved, historic, almost sacred pieces of art?

Forever

There's no denying it: our world values ancient treasures. It finds historic pieces of art and artifacts fascinating and worthy of the cost of protecting and preserving them. But what about you?

Well, the truth is that *your* value is not comparable to the treasures our world has stored up in museums. You are not an ancient artifact or a historic piece of art that people pay to get a glimpse of. Your face isn't known across the globe. Simply put, your worth is not like theirs. You are actually something *more*.

The *Mona Lisa* and all the possessions of the world are just things, things that will one day turn to dust. But you? You are more than a thing that will one day be gone forever, because you have a soul that was created to *live forever*.

You are immortal.

It's hard to wrap our minds around, but this is one of the greatest truths in this world. You. Will. Live. F o r e v e r. Wow, soak that in for a moment.

We Are Family

If the thought of your immortality isn't enough to make your head spin, there's still more.

God created us to live with him forever one day *in Heaven*. We are the only creation in this world to whom he granted this privilege, so it should come as no surprise that his relationship with us is unique and elevated.

God is not our slave driver, our puppeteer, or our genie—he is *our Father*. It is through his Son, Jesus's redeeming death on the Cross that we have the privilege of becoming adopted sons and daughters of the King of Heaven and Earth (Romans 8:15–17).

That's right: not only are you immortal, you are royalty.

If you can grasp even partially the truth of these two realities, then this is a game changer for the way you view yourself and others. Your worth is beyond measure. Their worth is beyond measure. You are not an ancient treasure—you are more. You are an immortal member of a royal family whose Father is the King of Heaven and Earth.

Today's Detox Challenge

Writing about man's immortality, C. S. Lewis said, "There are no *ordinary* people. You have never talked to a mere mortal. Nations, cultures, arts, civilizations—these are mortal, and their life is to ours as the life of a gnat. But it is immortals whom we joke with, work with, marry, snub, and exploit."[1]

In order to help himself see the invisible, immortal value of people, Leo challenged himself to spend one day focusing only on others' eyes. Today we want you to take on Leo's challenge. For the next twenty-four hours, if you are looking at someone, concentrate on the person's eyes and ask God to reveal to you the full worth of that person as one of his immortal sons and daughters.

And welcome to the end of the third day of the triggers challenge. Our sincere prayer is that you've been able to live up to it. If not, don't beat yourself up. Just call on your accountability partner for support and go to Confession if you need to.

We're not going to continue to remind you to take on the triggers challenge anew each day, but for the rest of this process, we hope you continue to avoid or set parameters around your triggers—because we hope that by now you've seen just how important it is to be free to love and be loved.

Day 9: People Are Not Things

My junior year in high school, I (Lisa) started dating a guy named Jack. About six weeks into our relationship it was Valentine's Day. For our special date he picked me up and took me back to his house, where I quickly realized that nobody else was home. After his homemade dinner (canned soup ... so classy, I know), we headed to the basement to watch a movie. Before the first scene even got underway, things started to get physical. Suddenly Jack paused and said to me, "I want to go all the way with you." I froze. "You know how I feel about that," I slowly replied. And he did know.

You see, Jack was supposed to be a good guy. We both went to Catholic schools, sometimes we even went to church together, and he knew all about my decision to remain a virgin until marriage. Yet here he was asking me to sleep with him. Things got awkward, we didn't talk about it, and then he took me home.

Shortly after that Jack showed up at my house to tell me he felt like we were "in a rut" and he "couldn't see the relationship going any further." Let me translate that for you. What he was basically saying was, "You won't sleep with me, so we are breaking up." In the moment, I couldn't believe that I was being dumped for not sleeping with him, but looking back, it all makes sense.

Jack was never really interested in me as a person, but he was interested in my body. He desired sexual gratification and his plan was to use me physically to get it. And when he didn't get it, I was no longer of use to him, so he tossed me aside and moved on to the next girl.

But at the time I was stunned. How could he be so heartless and self-centered? Had he really ever cared about me? Didn't he know that people are not things that others can use?

I Didn't Know Jack

When I told my friends about the breakup nobody was surprised. The conversations went something like this:

"Can you believe Jack dumped me because I wouldn't sleep with him?"

"Yep, duh, Lisa, Jack is a total player. Why are you shocked?"

"What?! Why didn't you tell me?"

"We did. You just didn't want to hear it."

You see, Jack went to a different high school than I did, so before we started dating all I really knew about him was that he had dated some popular girls at my school, and to be counted among them made me feel really special. And what I knew about myself before Jack and I started dating was that I *really* liked having a boyfriend. Boyfriends made me feel that I mattered, that I was important, because somebody wanted me.

When it comes right down to it, I was about as interested in Jack as a person as he was interested in me as a person. Although I wasn't after his body in the way that he was after mine, I sought the emotional gratification I got from having a boyfriend. To me, Jack was an ego-boosting void filler, and I was using him like a thing, just like he was using me.

I Did Know Jack

One of the more interesting aspects of my relationship with Lisa is that while I (Kevin) didn't know her for most of high school, we did know many of the same people. You see, Jack and I went to the same high school, and he sat next to me in third period. Two other guys she went to dances with were some of my best friends in grade school, and another became my best friend and was a groomsman in our wedding. If any of these guys had known that Lisa would one day be my wife, I can't help but wonder how that would have changed his view of her.

Whenever you are in a relationship with someone, that girl or guy is someone's daughter or son, sister or brother, and, if called to marriage, future wife or husband. If you can recognize this reality, I promise you that you will look at your date differently. Each individual is a person, not a thing.

Rightful Due

Karol Wojtyla, the man who would become Pope St. John Paul II, once wrote, "A person's rightful due is to be treated as an object of love, not as an object for use."[2] Lisa didn't love Jack when she was trying to use him to fill her emotional void. Jack didn't love Lisa when he was trying to use her to fill his sexual void. Neither of them was giving the other "a person's rightful due." They were both treating the other as an "object for use," and they were both violating each other's immense worth as immortal beings who were created to live forever.

So often the root cause of our relationship struggles comes down to our inability to see others as people with immortal souls who deserve to be loved, and not to see them as things that we can use. Making this shift is the key to finding what your heart is longing for in relationships. As you enter more deeply into this journey, we want you to keep this perspective in mind. People are not things to be used; they are to be loved as immortal sons and daughters of the Most High King.

Today's Detox Challenge

In your life, are you currently using people, either physically or emotionally? Is there a person who is currently using you, either physically or emotionally? Identifying and admitting that these kinds of relationships may exist in your life can be a difficult thing to do. However, if you want to move away from using or being used, you have to open your eyes to the truth of how you view and treat others and how others view and treat you.

Today's challenge is to write down in your journal the names of the people you may be using or who may be using you. You will come back to these names in a few days.

Day 10: Your Intellect, Will, and Passions

Every action that you perform in life is done because you think it will make you happy. You might go to a certain school so you can get a job, so you can make money, so you can buy things that you think will make you happy. You might enter into a dating relationship so you can have fun, so you can experience feelings of love, so you can be happy. Even when you are using people, either knowingly or unknowingly, you are doing it because you are searching for ways to be happy.

Have you ever given much thought to how you make decisions about which actions to take? As in, what does the process actually look like? If you simplify the progression of decision making, there are three elements, or faculties, as the Church calls them, that play into your decisions about what to do in any situation. They are your intellect, will, and passions.

The Intellect

God made you as a rational being, that is, a person who can reason. You can use critical thinking skills to arrive at logical conclusions about the world around you. The ability to reason is controlled by your intellect. Using your intellect, you can weigh options, solve complex problems, and create meaningful solutions to life's challenges. Utilizing your education, life experiences, and intuition, your ability to reason helps you make informed decisions that can lead to your happiness.

It is the job of the intellect to evaluate your physical and emotional experiences and ask, "Is this good?" For example, "Is viewing pornography good?" or, "Is it okay to flirt with my best friend's girlfriend/boyfriend?" When the intellect comes to a conclusion about something's goodness, it can determine the right thing to do.

The Will

God not only gave you an intellect that allows you to reason through situations, but he also gave you a will. The will is the faculty that chooses how to act in light of the conclusion the intellect has come to. Although the intellect can plan for the best course of action, the will has to consent to the plan in order for it to be acted upon.

Ultimately the will is free to do as it chooses, or, as you may have heard it said, you have free will. The will does not have to listen to the intellect; it can reject any conclusion that the intellect has made by simply not consenting to act in the way the intellect has determined to be best.

This freedom to choose is important, because without it, humans either would be like robots that blindly follow orders by force, or they would be like animals that have no control over their instinctual desires. As a human you are very different. You are the one who is in control of your actions; hence you are the one who is in control of the way you live your life.

The Passions

Finally, you have desires, or what philosophers and theologians call passions. On a basic level, your body desires the things you need physically, such as rest, food, water, and air. And on a deeper level, your heart desires the things you need emotionally, such as love, companionship, purpose, and a sense of belonging.

Each of these passions is good. In fact, God gave them to you for a reason. If you never had a desire to eat, you would starve to death. If no one ever had sexual desires, humans would stop procreating and die out. If we didn't desire to be in community with others, we would have to fend for ourselves, which would make it difficult to survive in this world. It is the job of your passions to see that these legitimate needs are heard and taken into consideration by the intellect.

Putting It All Together

If that seemed a bit complicated, bear with us as we try to break it down a bit more.

If you want to be happy, your intellect, will, and passions must all be working in harmony when you take action. The intellect, whose job it is to come up with the best thing to do, takes into consideration your physical and emotional passions and then informs the will to act in a certain way. Once the will has consented to acting upon the intellect's good decision, the action is carried out, the need is satisfied, and this leads to happiness.

Here is an example: You are hungry. Your passions let your intellect know that you are in need of something to eat and they would prefer you to make a pizza. Your intellect acknowledges the need for nourishment and you go to the kitchen to see what is available. There you find the frozen pizza that your passions are asking for, but you also find fruit. Now the inner dialogue begins:

Intellect: "We had fast food at lunch, so we should have fruit for a snack."

Passions: "Lame! We like pizza."

Intellect: "Too much grease in one day is not good for our body."

Passions: "But we've had a rough day. We deserve to have what we want."

Intellect: "We have had a rough day, but fruit will satisfy our hunger, and it is better for us."

After listening to this exciting dialogue, it's now time for your will to decide what to do. Pizza or fruit? In a perfect world it would listen to the good reasoning of your intellect and choose the fruit.

In a Perfect World

When the intellect, will, and passions all work together in this way, then happiness can follow. In our example, the passions were given the nourishment they asked for, and at the same time, the will consented to the intellect and made a good decision.

When we make decisions, we first have to seek out the truth using our intellect, then choose to pursue it without allowing our passions to prevent us from doing what we have discovered is the right thing.

Sounds simple enough, right? Well, not really. In a perfect world this would be easy, but we don't live in a perfect world, so it's not. You know from experience that sometimes your will doesn't consent to choose the fruit, and instead you end up eating the whole pizza. Now what? Well, that is where we will pick up tomorrow!

Today's Detox Challenge

Over the next twenty-four hours, we invite you to be conscious of what you are eating. Ask yourself if you are making healthy decisions when it comes to food. Try actively engaging your intellect in this area and be aware of what goes on during your thought process as you make choices about what you eat. Does your will readily consent to the suggestions of your intellect or do your passions make it difficult to make healthy decisions?

Day 11: When Things Go Wrong

Yesterday you looked at the intellect, will, and passions, and saw that when they are working in harmony, you make good decisions that can lead to your happiness. At the end of the chapter we pointed to the fact that this process isn't as straightforward as our pizza versus fruit example made it seem. So let's look at each faculty and see how exactly things can go wrong.

The Intellect

The intellect's job is to determine if something is good, and based upon that determination, it should come up with the right course of action. The problem is that the intellect doesn't *necessarily* know what is good.

At the end of his senior year of high school, Joseph and his on-again, off-again girlfriend broke up, but soon afterward they found themselves about to get back together ... again. Joseph reasoned with himself that if they were going to follow through with getting back together, then they needed to prove that they really loved each other by sleeping together, and that's exactly what they did. However, Joseph explained with regret, "It didn't sit well with me and a week later I broke up with her." This process perplexed Joseph because he felt as though he had given the situation a lot of thought, but in the end, he lamented his decision.

Was Joseph trying to be a player and just get game? No, he was doing what he thought to be right with the knowledge he had, and he was doing what he thought would make him happy. However, Joseph's intellect failed him because it didn't have all the right information regarding what would actually make him happy.

Surely, like Joseph, you can think of a time in your life when you thought through a decision, acted on the decision, and then later realized that you probably didn't do the right thing. Don't worry. You are not alone. We have all done this.

The Will

While your will's job is to consent to and properly execute decisions, it doesn't always act in the way you know it should: based upon the reasoning of your intellect. When your passions are pulling your will in another direction, it can be hard to consent to do what is right.

This was Therese's story. During Eucharistic Adoration at a conference, God's presence flooded over her and she felt drawn to start living a chaste life. For the rest of the academic year she succeeded, but when she came home from college for the summer, things became really hard. Therese started hanging out with her ex-boyfriend, and soon after she began sleeping with him again.

Therese explained to us, "I thought to myself, 'Now I know why it's wrong, and I'm still doing it, which makes me even more horrible.' Every time I'd leave his house after having sex, I'd bawl the whole way home. I was sick of myself and how I knew I was breaking God's heart."

Her challenge was moving from knowing what she wanted to do to being able to do it. This movement required an act of the will, or an active choice, not to engage in the behaviors that her intellect knew she no longer wanted to do.

The Passions

When it comes to decision making, the passions often try to hijack the job of the intellect by claiming that they are the ones to determine what is right and what will lead to happiness. It can be especially difficult to detect their sneaky ways, because in our world physical pleasures and emotional highs are often seen as the litmus test for happiness. This was the lie that Carlos bought into from a young age.

At thirteen, Carlos started engaging in sexual activities such as porn and masturbation. In his teenage years, he got into drugs and alcohol and eventually lost his virginity. By the time he was nineteen, he began to make a career out of his pleasure-seeking lifestyle by becoming a stripper and prostitute. (Yes, Carlos is now living his life for Jesus. Nobody is ever too far from the love and redemption of Jesus.)

"I thought I had everything," Carlos said, as he shook his head, "drugs, money, expensive cars, an apartment downtown, women at my call, but I was addicted to it all ... especially sex. It eventually got to a point where I couldn't go more than a few days without a sexual experience."

As time went by, Carlos hit a point in his life when he no longer wanted to live in such slavery, but he couldn't find a way out of it. "I did these things and I began to feel disgust toward them, even when I was in the trenches of it. I had to do ecstasy, smoke myself stupid, and drink to drown out my conscience."

Carlos's passions had taken such control over his intellect and will that he was enslaved by them and was no longer free to say no to them.

If reading these stories leaves you in a bit of despair, fear not: we are not all doomed. Fortunately, God has a plan for how to properly order your intellect, will, and passions, and tomorrow we will begin to uncover that plan.

Today's Detox Challenge

Today we invite you to spend some time thinking about which of the faculties you struggle with the most. Does your intellect have a hard time coming up with the right conclusions? Does your will have a hard time consenting to act in ways that you know are right? Are your passions constantly driving your

actions and silencing the voice of your intellect, which is trying
to lead you to the good?

Write down the areas where you struggle the most and take
them to prayer today, asking God to reveal to you ways in which
you can begin to set things straight.

Day 12: Choices

On Day 5 we introduced the concept of triggers, and we asked you to list the things in your life that trigger, or set you up for, sexual situations that you later regret. It's been one week since then, so now is a good time to ask: How is it going? Have you been able to avoid and/or set parameters for your triggers all week? If not, take it to prayer and, if need be, to Confession, then start again tomorrow. And don't be afraid to ask for backup from your accountability partner. (Your partner is walking with you along this journey, right? If not, send a reminder text right now asking for support.) Remember, no one is a lost cause, so take hope and keep fighting!

There are a few more things that will be really helpful for you to know about triggers, and now that you have an understanding of how your faculties of the intellect, will, and passions work, this is the perfect time to introduce them.

First, recall that your brain is designed to remember patterns. When it starts to notice a pattern, it assumes that you are repeating a particular behavior because you want to get good at it. For this reason, certain actions, environments, and routines work as triggers in your life that lead you to act in habitual ways.

So far you have only looked at how triggers can cause you to react outwardly with physical actions—hence our asking you to avoid certain triggers in order to prevent yourself from doing the things you don't want to do. What we have not mentioned yet is that there is a step that occurs between the trigger and the physical response: the inward response to a trigger.

An Inward Response

All day your body is receiving information through its senses by seeing, hearing, smelling, tasting, and touching a variety of stimuli. Each of these bits of information acts as a trigger and provides an opportunity for your passions, which are your physical and emotional desires, to respond in a variety of ways.

Let's say you meet a new person at your school or work, which immediately triggers a response of attraction. That feeling of fascination that welled up inside of you is not something you can control; it is something that happens to you. In that moment, the experience of attraction is neither right nor wrong; as *The Catechism of the Catholic Church* (CCC) puts it, "In themselves passions are neither good or evil" (CCC 1767).

Your passions, which include your experiences of attraction, happen naturally and unintentionally and are thus morally neutral. What matters is what you choose to do with those passions. You can either use them to lead you to what is true, good, and beautiful, or to what is fake, bad, and ugly.

After seeing this person who entices you, your intellect and will begin working and decide what to do with that attraction. The intellect may think, "Okay, I'm dating someone, so I shouldn't go there." If the will consents, then together they do not indulge in the idea of taking the attraction beyond the sensation that happened to you. Bravo! You have chosen to do something good with that attraction and used it as an opportunity to strengthen your resolve to be faithful to the person you are currently dating.

But what does it look like when the attraction leads you to act upon something wrongly? Well, you could allow your passions, which are excited about this new interest, to run over your intellect and act upon the attraction anyway. Now you have allowed your passions to call the shots and have opened the door to something that could lead you to being unfaithful to the person you are currently in a relationship with.

You Have a Choice

As we can see in the above scenario, there is a difference between experiencing an attraction and acting upon it. Having the attraction is not wrong, but acting upon it can be. The key is recognizing that *you have a choice*. Just because a stimulus triggers you to want to react in a particular way doesn't mean you have to do it. You. Have. A. Choice. You have an intellect that can reason through the situation, you have a will that can consent to doing the right thing, and you do not have to give in to passions that leave you with feelings of regret and disappointment.

What's even better is that because you have a choice, you can actually retrain yourself to react differently when a certain trigger is presented to you. You can create new responses to triggers, responses that will lead your passions to desire what is good, true, and beautiful, as opposed to what is bad, fake, and ugly.

The goal isn't to repress your desires. The goal is to transform them.

What you need to accomplish that is a little something called virtue. With the help of virtue, you can learn to order your intellect, will, and passions to work in harmony, so that your responses to triggers can lead to good decisions and actions that can help lead you to the happiness you're searching for. That's where we'll pick up tomorrow.

Today's Detox Challenge

For today's challenge we propose that you take out your journal and turn to your page of triggers. Above your triggers write: "You have a choice." Then, over these next few weeks, begin to work on formulating alternative responses to your triggers. For example, in the past, if someone texted you something inappropriate, your response may have been to reply. What could you do as an alternative? Could you delete the text without responding? As you continue to find alternatives that work for specific triggers, write them next to the trigger and begin to *choose* to use it.

If coming up with and following through on alternative responses seems overwhelming and difficult, don't give in to despair. You won't be alone in those moments. Say a prayer when you have an opportunity to choose, and let Christ be your strength. He's brought you to this point and put it on your conscience to make these changes, and he will not abandon you when you need him.

Day 13: Virtue

In order for your intellect, will, and passions to be able to do their jobs, they have to be properly formed, working as they were made to work. As we already learned, your intellect doesn't necessarily know what is right and can make bad decisions when it doesn't have accurate information. Your will doesn't always listen to your intellect and consent to the things it suggests. And your pleasure-seeking passions don't always know what is right, despite the fact that they think they do. The answer to all these dilemmas is virtue.

But what exactly is virtue?

Forty Days of Terror

Remember the story of David and Goliath? It's the one in which a small Israelite boy goes head-to-head with a giant Philistine warrior in an all-or-nothing battle.

We aren't sure exactly how big the Philistine giant Goliath was, but we do know that he was significantly taller and stronger than any of the Israelites. We also know that after Goliath in his many pounds of armor challenged the Israelites, they "were dismayed and greatly afraid" (1 Samuel 17:11). At first, no one would step forward to face him. For forty days Goliath challenged them, until David finally convinced the king to let him fight. You may know the end of the story—with just five stones and a slingshot, David defeated the giant.

When No One Was Looking

God's hand was surely with David at the battle, but David's skill didn't just randomly appear that day. Before David's epic battle, he was a shepherd boy. That's right—he watched sheep all day. It sounds like an uneventful life, until you consider that a shepherd doesn't just stare at sheep, he protects them. During his days keeping watch, David was practicing with his slingshot, so that if a predator came along, like a lion or a bear, he would be ready to smite the beast, which is exactly what he did on several occasions (1 Samuel 17:34).

When no one was watching, David was perfecting the skills he needed to use a slingshot with ease and precision, and when he had to use those skills as a shepherd, he was also getting into the habit of being brave. Although he couldn't have foreseen just how badly he would one day need these two abilities, he was cultivating the habits necessary to do the right thing at the right time in the right way, which enabled him to save his people.

The Moral Virtues

The *Catechism* defines the moral virtues[3] as "firm attitudes, stable dispositions, habitual perfections of intellect and will that govern our actions, order our passions, and guide our conduct according to reason and faith" (CCC 1804). Simply put, a virtue is a habit of doing the right thing, which is necessary for your intellect, will, and passions to work well.

The moral virtues are each categorized under one of the four Cardinal Virtues: prudence, justice, fortitude, and temperance. Let's take a look at them.

> **Prudence:** Prudent people make good decisions based upon their informed knowledge of right and wrong. They can clearly see the truth of a situation and act on this truth because they know how to reason. In order for the intellect to do its job, it needs the virtue of prudence.

> **Justice:** The world understands justice to be what others owe us, but traditionally justice is about what we owe others and God. A person who practices justice is fair and looks at others as people with dignity who deserve to be treated with respect.

When it is tough to do the right thing, justice can particularly help our will consent to the correct choice.

Fortitude: People who have fortitude are courageous. When it comes to disordered passions, denying them takes fortitude. Fear can grip people and lead them to believe that the momentary pleasure they gain from indulging their passions is as good as it gets and that if they deny their passions, then they will be left without any relief from the difficulties of this world. When people possess fortitude they can overcome fear and courageously do what is right.

Temperance: Temperate people can restrain themselves. They have self-control over their physical and emotional desires, not the other way around. Temperate people control their passions, rather than their passions controlling them.

One of the sub-virtues of temperance is chastity, which is especially important in gaining the freedom to love and be loved. You've probably heard the word before, but we want to give a concrete definition of it, to make sure we are on the same page. The *Catechism* defines chastity as "the successful integration of sexuality within the person and thus the inner unity of man in his bodily and spiritual being" (CCC 2337). This means that chastity is not simply refraining from sexual intercourse. Rather, it is an integration of sexuality that frees us to love rightly. This is how we want you to think of chastity. It is the virtue that gives you the habits you need to be free to love and be loved.

Practice Makes Progress

The virtues of prudence, justice, fortitude, and temperance will help guide you to order your intellect, will, and passions properly. When you practice virtue, you are able to know the truth and act accordingly, while taking the legitimate needs of your passions into consideration without allowing them to take control. It is only with practice that you can truly develop virtuous habits, but once you have learned them, then you are free to perform them.

Think of it this way: Anyone is "free" to pound on the keys of a piano, but if you have not been trained in the art of playing the piano, then you will only make noise. Only the person who has dedicated time and effort to learn how to play is truly free to make music.

This same principle can be applied to any area of life, even dating relationships. Any single person is free, or allowed, to enter into a relationship with someone, but if you want to be free, or truly able, to love and be loved, then you must gain the skills—or virtues—that are necessary to do so.

Facing the Giant

Building the virtue of chastity so you can be free to love and be loved may seem like facing the giant Goliath. It's big, intimidating, and scary. Like the Israelites, you may be afraid to confront it because defeat appears certain.

But if you learn from David's story, then you will know you have nothing to fear. The Lord will be with you and strengthen you as you take on this challenge. If you combine his strength with your willingness to practice virtue in little things, then you will have what it takes to claim victory when you are tested in big things.

Today's Detox Challenge

Today we invite you to choose a way to practice one of the Cardinal Virtues. For example, if you want to work on the virtue of temperance, deny your passions and take a cold shower. Or if you want to work on the virtue of justice, give others their due by helping a person in need today.

Day 14: Love vs. Use

With great resentment, George was saving sex for marriage. From a young age, his Catholic upbringing told him that this was the right thing to do, so he did it. However, he still got as physical as he could with his girlfriend, Madison, without *technically* crossing the forbidden line.

After several months of this, George admitted, "It got to a point where when I was alone with my girlfriend, all I could think about was when we were going to do stuff. I couldn't just enjoy *her*. And it was getting harder and harder to say no to going all the way."

Eventually George and Madison's relationship broke off. Around that time, George started to learn about God's plan for love and relationships and everything clicked. He no longer wanted to push the line; instead he actually *wanted* to live the virtue of chastity.

Everything was going well for George until several months later, when he reconnected with Madison and one night they fell into their old habit of messing around. Feeling a profound sense of defeat and shame when it was over, George knew that he had yielded to using Madison—so the next day he immediately went to Confession with a resolve to start again. But that very night he allowed himself to get into the exact same situation he had been in the night before.

As things began to heat up, a thought suddenly stopped George in his tracks: "I knew I had two options: choose to 'enjoy' her selfishly or choose *not* to use her as a toy and die to myself. By the grace of God, I chose the latter, and immediately my perception of her totally changed. I could see the beauty of her soul, and I felt a love for her I never had before."

George went on to describe that before that night he thought that the physical intimacy he shared with his girlfriend was his way of loving her, but really it was just his way of using her for his own enjoyment. It wasn't until that night, when he was able to say no to using her body, that he was free to love her for the first time. To his surprise, his sacrifice for her didn't lead to repression and unhappiness. Rather, he felt fully alive.

Willing the Good

St. Thomas Aquinas once said, "To love is to will the good of another" (CCC 1766). As you read earlier, the will is the faculty that chooses how you act. To say that to love is to *will* the good of another means that to love is to *choose* the good of another, or to want what's best for the other person. Not only does this kind of love *want* what's best for another, but it also *acts* in ways that reflect that desire, even if this requires making sacrifices. George displayed this kind of love that wills the good of the other when he made a sacrifice for Madison in choosing not to treat her like a thing by using her for a physical high.

Ultimately love is a choice; it's something that you choose to do. Choosing to love in this way can be difficult, so in order to succeed, you need your relationships to be based in virtue, which will allow you to build the skills and habits necessary to be free to love and be loved.

Virtuous Relationships

Relationships that are based in virtue are founded on the pursuit of the common goal of living a good and virtuous life together. They are not concerned with personal gain; rather, they're concerned with both parties becoming their best selves. In order for a relationship to be truly virtuous, each person must allow the higher goal of pursuing virtue together to lead his or her actions. And although they might not always reach this ideal, it is at the forefront of their minds and something for which they are continually striving.

Let's say a relationship suddenly became long-distance with little communication. Would the lack of the physical presence of the other take with it all the good feelings? Or what if a dating couple who has been sleeping together for months stopped being intimate due to an illness or because they decided to be chaste? Would the relationship fall apart?

In these situations, if the lack of a useful or pleasurable element in addition to the necessity for sacrifice dooms the relationship to its end, then it's a sure sign that it was based on use. If taking away good feelings or sexual gratification remove love, then true love was never there.

The Virtuous Love Test: Is It Love or Use?

To find out if your relationships are striving for virtuous love or if they are based upon use, simply ask yourself, "Is my relationship based on willing the other's good and mutual growth in virtue—or not?" (*Please* keep in mind that these commitments must be two-sided because if they are not, then you might not be using someone, but the other person is probably using you.) If your relationship is based on willing each other's good, then you are probably on track. If not, then you have some thinking to do.

Today's Detox Challenge

Remember that list we invited you to write down on Day 9? The list of people you may be using or who may be using you? Look back at that list now and use the virtuous love test to evaluate these relationships. Are they based on virtuous love or use? Are the people on your list concerned with willing your good or getting something from you? Are you concerned with willing their good or getting something from them?

If you've realized that you are using someone or being used by someone, take these relationships to prayer and maybe even to the person who is keeping you accountable, or a trusted friend or mentor. Ask the Lord to show you where to go from here.

P.S. We've found that people aren't trying to be careless and intentionally use others. Our goal here is not to try to make you feel like a horrible person or to imply that a person who is using you is the scum of the earth. More often than not, it's a lack of understanding that leads people to use others. Now that you know the difference between love and use, we hope you strive to choose love.

Discussion Questions for Week 2

1. What do you think the relationship is between the way you view yourself and others and the ability to love authentically? What obstacles make it difficult to view yourself and others the way God does?

2. The intellect, will, and passions play a huge role in our relationships. How would you describe these three faculties?

3. What stood out to you as you learned about the intellect, will, and passions? Which one do you think you struggle with most?

4. Often our culture tells us that love is a feeling or that falling in love happens by fate. How does realizing that love is a choice change the way you view relationships?

5. Virtue is a pivotal way to make incremental steps toward authentic love. How have you seen the effects of virtue in your own life in the past? What are some ways that you can use this week's lessons to love authentically today?

6. Knowing the difference between love and use is a key principle in living out authentic love. What are some differences between love and use?

WEEK 3: PHYSICAL PASSIONS

Welcome to Week 3! Last week you discovered that you are an immortal member of a royal family who should not be treated like a thing for others to use either physically or emotionally. You learned that your faculties of the intellect, will, and passions need to be directed by virtue in order to make true happiness possible. And you were invited to take the virtuous love test to see if the relationships in your life are based on love or use. We will be coming back to these topics throughout the remainder of this journey, so try to keep them fresh in your mind.

Over the next two weeks we will be diving deeper into the physical and emotional passions you experience in your life. To begin, this week we will look at your physical passions, that is, your desire for sexual intimacy.

Day 15: Writing the Rules

Yesterday we shared the story of George, who, with great resentment, was trying to remain a *technical* virgin. "I knew of God's love for me," George said, "but I still didn't fully follow his rules for sexuality because I didn't really believe that would lead to my happiness."

Perhaps you can relate to George's dilemma. You know that God loves you, and you know that he asks you not to cross certain sexual lines, yet you still cross them.

It's an important dilemma to ponder because (let's be honest) it's unlikely that you will be able to live chastely just because that's what you are supposed to do and because being one of the "good kids" is your highest aspiration. Yep, not going to work, at least not for the long haul. For chastity to stick, you have to believe that it's actually worth it and that it's truly the best thing for you and for others.

Rules

As a homeschooled kid, Daniel spent most of his grade school days at his kitchen table learning the rules of grammar and math, which specified that there are certain procedures that he had to obey. Sentences must have a subject and a verb, the circumference of a circle needed to equal 360 degrees, and so on. It was in this same matter-of-fact way that he was taught to follow the rules of his Faith. Sin separates us from God. Sexual intercourse is a sacred act that is reserved for the confines of marriage, et cetera.

After graduating from eighth grade homeschool, Daniel headed off to an all-boys high school with this knowledge in hand. At his prep school, no one ever challenged the validity of what he had learned about grammar and math. However, he was challenged on what he had learned about his Faith, and when his rote answers didn't seem convincing enough to himself or to others, he started to doubt whether they were worth following.

"I got tired of breaking up with these beautiful girls over the morals that I had clung to," Daniel recalled. "I felt like my morals were being pried away from me because I didn't have good reasons for not drinking, smoking weed, or getting with girls. I didn't have anything that was super convincing for not doing these things. What seemed more convincing was to do the opposite of what I was taught."

As Daniel's moral foundation slowly eroded, he eventually gave up altogether and dove into a lifestyle of partying on weekends and trying to hook up with girls. At first, no longer being the obstinate guy who was always holding out came with some pleasurable rewards, but the contradiction between his lifestyle and the faith he pretended to hold on to started to get to him. It was at this juncture that Daniel decided to get rid of the hypocrisy by becoming agnostic.

Writing His Own Rules

With his set of religious, moral rules tossed aside, Daniel began to make decisions based on his own personal experiences and the experiences of those around him. In the beginning he tried going the "nice guy" route and only slept with girls he was in a serious relationship with. After giving sufficient time to a relationship, he and his girlfriend would sleep together and "play house," as he described it. At first the satisfaction of being in a secure, committed relationship felt awesome, but when a breakup was on the horizon, Daniel knew that pain was coming.

"When you are having sex with somebody it covers up so much stuff in the relationship—it's like you are floating on a cloud. For a while you can get away with breaking God's rules as you suspend reality, but there you are ten miles up and then the high wears off, the cloud evaporates, and you crash. It's brutal."

Changing the Rules

With the memory of the crash in the front of Daniel's mind, he tried a different approach to girls, one that wouldn't require so much giving and would avoid the potential of getting hurt ... i.e., the casual hookup. Daniel explained, "I found that when you do break up it's too hard, so I learned to hook up with girls and then keep moving quickly so as not to string it out."

But even this approach left him feeling uneasy. "Hooking up is so glorified in the media and male society. There is all of this positive reinforcement that comes with scoring, and guys want the respect of their peers, so we just talk about the positives of it." However, Daniel explained, casually sleeping with someone wasn't really a positive experience. "When it was just about sex, there was an emptiness and uneasiness about it and I felt an immense amount of performance anxiety. I would be so worried about whether or not she was enjoying it. When it was over, I'd think, 'That's not right, that's not what I really wanted.' I tried to justify the feelings as a Catholic guilt complex, but it never went away."

When the World Doesn't Deliver

Have you been there? Have you had that feeling of "that's not right, that's not what I really wanted"? Think back to some times when you've crossed lines. Can you remember the mixed feelings? In the moment maybe it felt good and it was fun, but how about the next day, when you were alone again in your room and that person was gone? Remember those feelings and sit with them for a moment. Was the result of that experience really what you were hoping for? Now think about a committed relationship that you've been in. Perhaps at first the relationship felt full of love and satisfaction, but how about when you broke up? In that instance, did you get what you had truly been longing for?

When we can admit that what we got wasn't really what we wanted, our first inclination is to find a logical reason for why it didn't work the way we planned. "It was the wrong person; our personalities just didn't mesh." "The timing just wasn't right. He was coming off a relationship, and we jumped in too soon." "We didn't technically sleep together, but next time I'll make sure I'm not half drunk." "Maybe if I didn't have a Catholic guilt complex, or if people weren't so prudish, then I wouldn't have issues with letting go of my inhibitions and enjoying myself."

You can come up with all kinds of reasons for why it didn't work out, but consider this: Could it be that the real problem was not the person, the timing, the circumstances, Catholic guilt, or anything of the sort? Perhaps the reason it didn't feel quite right was because of the sexual acts themselves. Perhaps you weren't following *God's* rules for love, dating, and sex but were following *your* rules?

Today's Detox Challenge

Today we ask you to think back to a time when you wrote your own rules for love, dating, and sex. What kinds of feelings and thoughts came from that experience? Write them down. Now reflect on these last two weeks when you have been striving to live according to God's rules. What kinds of feelings and thoughts have come from this experience? Write them down, too. Compare the two lists. Which list do you want to experience on a consistent basis?

Day 16: How It Should Be

The purpose of a car is to get us from point *a* to point *b*. Let's say you are in a rush and you see that there is a quicker way to get to where you want to go, but there's a big lake in the way. "Eh," you think to yourself, "who are they to tell me where I can and can't go?" So, to assert your freedom to do what you want, when you want, and how you want, you drive your car straight into the lake that is blocking your way. Naturally, you begin to sink. Now you are annoyed because your car didn't provide you with the outcome you desired because, after all, you should be free to do what you want.

Sounds ridiculous, right? Yet how often do we live our lives like this? We desire a certain outcome and we want it to happen on our terms, but it doesn't always work out. Why? Well, in the car illustration, things didn't work because the purpose of the car was violated. Cars cannot drive on water; they were made to drive on the ground. And just as a car has a purpose, so does sex. When we violate the purpose of sex, things tend not to turn out as desired.

Yesterday we looked at how this played out in Daniel's life. Daniel tried to come up with his own rules and purpose for his physical desires, but in the end he knew in the depths of his heart that his approach was not right. When he realized this, he began to search for new answers. To understand what Daniel discovered, we need to look at two things: first, the purpose of sex, and second, what sex tells us about the love of God.

The Purpose of Sex

Throughout the ages the Church has always confirmed that sexual intercourse has a twofold purpose: unity and procreation.

The procreative end of sexual intimacy is the means by which we continue to populate the earth; in other words, sex is designed to make babies. The sexual act is also designed to bring two people together in a united bond of love. God knew that marriage would sometimes be tough, so he intended the one-flesh union to be a way to help spouses stay unified in difficult times. Essentially, sex is for bonding and babies.

Although sex has some very practical purposes, it also has a spiritual aim. It teaches us something about the love of God. To understand *what* that is we need first to look at *who* God is.

Reflections

God is not just a Divine Person; rather, he is three Divine Persons—God the Father, God the Son, and God the Holy Spirit—who are one in Being (cf. CCC 253). Together these three Persons of the Trinity make up an eternal communion, or "common union." As such, each Person of the union gives of himself to the others out of love. God the Father lovingly makes a total gift of himself to God the Son, and in return God the Son lovingly makes a total gift of himself to God the Father. God the Holy Spirit proceeds from this eternal exchange of self-giving, unified love. In one sense, the Holy Spirit is the eternal fire of love between the Father and Son, and this love is so powerful and real that it *is* a Person.

Now, consider how human love reflects this divine love: When a married man and woman come together to make a total gift of self to each other in the act of sex, the result of their love sometimes comes in the form of a third person, a baby. In a limited way, their act of coming together in the marital embrace reflects the love of the Trinity. This is not to say that the Trinity is sexual, but rather that our sexuality has a divine design.

The Love of the Trinity

While the Trinity is and always will be a theological mystery that can never be fully defined, explained, or understood, there are four attributes of the love of the Trinity that can provide us with a context for beginning to understand the ways in which we are called to love in sexual acts.

First of all, the love that is shared among the Trinity is *free*. It is a love that is freely given and does not expect anything in return. Second, it is *faithful*. The Father will never abandon the Son and the Son will never abandon the Father. Third, the love of the Trinity is *total*. It does not hold anything back. God the Father does not pick and choose which parts of himself he is going to share with the Son; rather, he gives him everything and vice versa. Lastly, the love of the Trinity is *life-giving* in the perpetual exchange of love among the three Divine Persons, which spills out into creation.

Marital Love

The marital embrace of sexual love should reflect this same kind of free, faithful, total, and life-giving love.[1]

Love between a husband and a wife should be *free*. They should enter into the marriage union of their own free will, choosing to give themselves to each other freely. The love between a husband and wife should be *faithful*. In their wedding vows, husband and wife commit to entering into an exclusive covenant that does not leave room for cheating on or abandoning one's spouse. The love between husband and wife should be *total*. It should not be based upon conditions, such as "I'll love you if … ," "I'll love you when … ," or "I'll love you so long as.…" It should be a complete love in which no part of oneself is withheld. Finally, the love between a husband and wife should be *life-giving*, both physically in the form of openness to children, and emotionally as they bond with each other through the sharing of life, particularly in the marital embrace of sex.

When marital love is free, faithful, total, and life-giving, then the twofold purpose of sex—procreation and unity—flows naturally, because when two people love like the Trinity, *there is no room for use.*

Today's Detox Challenge

We have already invited you to pick a particular person on earth to be your accountability partner and cheer you along this journey. Today we invite you to pick someone in Heaven to do the same by choosing a patron saint of your pursuit to love virtuously.

A patron saint is a person in Heaven whom you ask to pray for you in a special way. Having a particular saint watching out for you gives you someone to ask for strength through prayer at any given moment.

If you are not sure which saint to choose, look up St. Maria Goretti or St. Aloysius Gonzaga, who are both patrons of chastity and purity. Once you've chosen a patron, we suggest you write the name of your patron saint on the front page of your journal, followed by "Pray for me!" And don't forget, you can repeat this phrase as often as necessary when you are struggling. In those times, your patron's prayers can help give you the added graces you need.

Day 17: Problems and Solutions

Yesterday, we began looking at God's purpose for sex (unity and procreation). Today, we are going to look at how these purposes can only properly be met in the lifelong bond of marriage, which strives to reflect the free, faithful, total, and life-giving love of the Trinity.

Problem #1: Non-Committal Bonding

Oxytocin is a hormone secreted during physical intimacy, childbirth, and when a mother is nursing an infant.[2] It acts like superglue and bonds two people together, which is quite practical for the ups and downs of family life. However, when oxytocin is secreted outside of marriage, trouble ensues as people are bonding in a way that is meant for a lifelong commitment where no lifelong commitment has been made.

The bonding effects of oxytocin are what keep people in bad relationships. It's the reason why the crash hurts so badly when a couple who have been sleeping together break up. It's what makes it so uncomfortable for people to see someone they randomly hooked up with. These are all natural emotions that our conscience uses to cry out to us, "Something is not right!" In the end, sex outside of marriage tampers with the God-given, unitive nature of the marital act.

Problem #2: Rejecting Life

From a young age, most of us have been taught that if we are going to engage in sex outside of marriage then we need to make sure to have "safe sex," that is, sex that prevents babies from being conceived. The rationale of this line of thinking is that having a child with someone is a lifelong commitment and you wouldn't want to make that commitment with just anyone. So the safe thing to do is to cut off the possibility of conceiving new life. This approach to sex poses a problem because sex that cuts off the possibility of a baby does not reflect the love of the Trinity.

To say to someone that you want the bonding benefits of physical intimacy but not the babies that might come with it is a rejection of *total* love, because one's fertility is a part of who one is. Essentially saying "I'll take all of you except your fertility" is not striving to imitate the total love of the Trinity. This is why the Church emphatically teaches that contraception is a violation of God's intended purpose for sexual unity. The love of the Trinity produces new life, and thus the love between a man and a woman should be open to doing the same. Certainly not every sexual act *will* result in new life, but in order for sex to be a total act of love, it must at least be open to allowing God, the author of life, to bring about new life if he so chooses.[3]

The Solution

If the purposes of sexual intimacy are violated, it will never result in the outcome that we hope for. Just like trying to drive a car across a lake won't get you where you want to go, neither will deviating from God's design for sex liberate you to fulfill your sexual desires according to *your* rules.

The good news is that there is plenty of reason for hope, because if we do follow God's design for sexual love, then it is possible for us to love as we were made to love. God's rules don't bind us and confine us. Rather, they free us to live as we were made to live and to love as we were made to love—and that is true liberation.

Imagine how truly liberating sex would be if you knew that the love you were receiving was *freely* and unconditionally given without expecting anything in return. Imagine if you knew that your beloved would be *faithful* to you and would not dump you for a "better option." Imagine if you knew that you were *totally* loved as you are and that who you are was enough in the eyes of your beloved. Imagine if you had no reason to fear the natural *life-giving* results of sexual love.

Would you feel safe and secure in a love like that? Would you feel free to love and be loved in a love like that? We believe you would. Free, faithful, total, and life-giving sex within the bonds of marriage makes secure love possible because married sex allows couples to love the way that God intended them to love.

Don't Lose Hope

We know that what we just laid out for you is a high ideal. It can even seem impossible. After all, we are imperfect, broken human beings. We make mistakes, we can be selfish, and we don't always do what we know we should do. This is all true, but it should not lead you to despair.

Remember that the only way you can even come close to living up to these standards is through the strength and grace of God. Ultimately, he is the one who will make it possible for you to strive to imitate the way he loves. Remember, too, that human love will not always live up to the standards that we have been given, but imagine how different things would be if you were at least *trying*. Could you ask more from a marriage than for both spouses to strive to love each other with such a profound love?

Today's Detox Challenge

Ten days ago we proposed that you set a goal to accomplish during this forty-day journey. Are you making progress? Have you reached your goal already? Have you forgotten about it altogether? You are going through an intense experience and you need to be sure you're giving yourself time and space to relax as you process it. Working toward your goal can help you do that. We hope today you resolve to take the next step in accomplishing that goal and be proud of how far you've come!

Day 18: Affection or Arousal

It's 10:00 A.M. on Saturday and you've just been sent the following text from your sweetie: "I've got a surprise planned for tonight, pick you up at 5."

"Fantastic!" you think to yourself and quickly rearrange your day for the special night.

At 5:00 P.M. sharp you are ready to go and your date is at your door. After a short drive, you arrive at an upscale buffet that has just opened in your city. Having eaten a light lunch in anticipation of the night's events, you are thrilled to see that dinner is an all-you-can-eat buffet. Your waiter seats you at a cozy corner booth and as he explains the different buffet stations, your excitement about the feast heightens with each word he speaks. As soon as he's finished you practically race to the buffet line and fill your extra-large dish to the brim. When your plate can handle no more, you resolve to come back for seconds later.

Upon returning to the table, your date greets you with a curious expression.

"You know, I'm actually not too hungry. Let's just forget dinner tonight," your date tells you while getting up to leave.

Not knowing quite what to do, you abandon your much-desired dinner at the table and angrily follow. "What is this about?" you think to yourself. "Between the invitation, bringing me to a restaurant, and letting me fill up my plate, I thought we were actually going to eat! Now I'm starving and we're abruptly walking away from it all?"

Everything *But*

A question we often hear is, "I get that sex should be saved for marriage, but why can't we do everything *but*? If I'm still technically a virgin, isn't that good enough?"

The problem with the "everything but" approach to sexual intimacy is the same problem that came up in the above scenario. Everything leading up to that moment made it seem as if you were about to fulfill your passions, which were crying out for satisfaction, but the true purpose of your actions was never fulfilled.

The culmination of your excursion should have been actually eating dinner. Likewise, the culmination of sexual arousal, whether it is passionate kissing, sexual touching, or anything else, should be *sex*. As we have seen, sex is only good and appropriate within the context of marriage. So it follows that acts that bring about sexual arousal should be reserved for marriage as well.

Outside of marriage, trying to arouse someone sexually or get aroused by someone sexually violates the nature of sexual love. It leads to disappointment and confusion as your body is getting prepared for something that it doesn't intend to bring to fulfillment. Arousing someone sexually without the intent of truly loving the person with a free, faithful, total, and life-giving love is using someone for self-seeking gratification.

Let's be very clear. What we're saying is that *all* acts that are meant to arouse someone sexually should be reserved for marriage because it is only within marriage that sexual love can actualize its true purpose.

Now, before you think that the next chapter is going to be on how to get your parents to set up the perfect arranged marriage for you, let's dig a bit deeper.

Arousal vs. Affection

Not every physical act must necessarily be an act that is meant to arouse another. You can kiss your grandma on the cheek, hold the hand of a scared child, or hug a friend goodbye, and none of these physical encounters would be considered acts that were meant to cause sexual arousal. Rather, they would be seen as acts that were meant to show affection. In the same way, you can extend acts of affection to someone you are dating without the intention of turning those acts into occasions for arousal.

Acts of affection have a place in the dating equation, and it is good and appropriate for a dating couple to interact with each other at a proper physical level. This allows the couple to learn how to order their passions rightly through the guidance of the intellect and will. It also allows them to integrate the virtue of chastity into their lives and to learn self-mastery. *Even in marriage* it is important not to sexualize every physical act, as this can lead to someone mistakenly seeing his or her spouse as an object that exists for the purpose of fulfilling physical passions.

How Far Is Too Far?

With this mindset, the "how far is too far" question becomes less confusing. If you want to know how far is too far, just evaluate your intentions. Are your actions seeking to arouse the person sexually or are your actions seeking to love the person affectionately?

The primary intention of an act of affection should come from a desire to will the good of another and act in a way that will lead the person closer to Christ. These are the kinds of intentions that will prevent us from using others. So if you are ever unsure about your physical interactions with your boyfriend or girlfriend, just ask yourself, "Does this action desire what's best for him or her and bring us both closer to Christ?"

Has messing around in a dark room with your boyfriend or girlfriend ever been about what's best for him or her? More often than not, it's just about doing what feels good. Has making out with a random person or hooking up with your ex ever brought you closer to Christ? Be honest, has it? We doubt it, so it's no wonder we feel disappointed, hurt, confused, and gypped by acts that don't point back to the Author of Love. It's no wonder we know that there has to be more.

Today's Detox Challenge

Today we suggest you ask yourself when it is that affection turns into arousal for you. The "how far is too far" line for hand-holding, hugging, kissing, or nonsexual touching will vary from person to person. We know some dating couples who chose not to engage in any physical touching for a time, while others held hands and briefly kissed good night. In both situations the couples were able to be affectionate virtuously.

The key to their success was that both parties were honest about their individual limits. If a couple is alone, the tipping point for one of them might be cozying up on a couch, and for the other it might just be *the couch*. Knowing each other's limits ensures that certain temptations aren't unintentionally presented.

Where are you at? What lines do you need to draw at this time so you do not cross from an act of affection to acts of arousal? We invite you to write down in your journal what you need to do now to ensure that your physical actions are ordered toward love and not lust or use. A tip: if you are unsure, lean toward the conservative side; it is better to err away from your line than toward it.

Day 19: XXX

Xavier

Xavier began looking at porn in the seventh grade. He loved seeing the images and videos. They made him feel good inside—so he dove in.

Later on, he found out that viewing pornography was a sin. So out of fear of going to Hell, he would confess after viewing. He knew he needed to stop, but he didn't want to. That feeling of "love" and the enjoyment of watching had him hooked. He carried this habit into high school and eventually his lust spilled into his dating relationships as well.

He wondered, "What is wrong with me? Why can't I stop?"

Monica

In high school, Monica struggled with chastity in her dating relationships. After her conversion, she was able to draw lines with guys and control her triggers. In college, Monica's faith really started to take off. She dedicated herself more to the Lord and became a leader in her campus parish. Everything was great, except for the secret she didn't want anyone to know about: she struggled with masturbation and sexual fantasies that were fueled by an addiction to pornography.

While she tried a few different ways to overcome these challenges, she still fell into her same old patterns. Why wasn't anything working?

Breaking It Down

Our culture is absolutely saturated with sexuality. Ads, movies, and TV shows constantly put sex front and center. When all this is combined with the good and natural sex drive that God gave us, it is no surprise that so many people, even very committed Catholics, struggle in the areas of pornography, fantasies, and masturbation. If this is you, know that you are not alone in this struggle.

Let's break down the three different challenges:

With fantasies, we create an unrealistic or improbable image in our mind (often lustful in nature) that helps meet sexual desire in an illegitimate way. Although the desire is real, the fantasies are not, and they can often lead our hearts to a place we know we shouldn't go.

With masturbation, we seek out physical pleasure. God gave us a sex drive and a desire to procreate, and we want to express this with our bodies, but masturbation does so in a way that's ultimately not healthy.

Pornography, whether videos or images, takes both fantasies and masturbation to a whole new level. Porn is like pouring gasoline on a fire. It takes our own thoughts and sex drives and ignites them. When this happens, things can get out of control in a hurry.

The Why

As we face these challenges, it's important to ask the question: So why are these things wrong again? Our society tells us that they are perfectly fine, normal, and healthy.

Simply knowing that our faith prohibits them usually isn't enough for most people. We need to understand why they don't help us fulfill authentic love.

The Christian writer, C.S. Lewis, once wrote: "For me the real evil of masturbation would be that it … sends the man back into the prison of himself, there to keep a harem of imaginary brides. And this harem, once admitted, works against his ever getting out and really uniting with a real woman. For the harem is always accessible, always subservient, calls for no sacrifices or adjustments, and can be endowed with erotic and psychological attractions which no real woman can rival." [4]

So, yeah, C. S. Lewis doesn't pull any punches. While he is specifically addressing masturbation, it's not hard to see how his wisdom easily applies to porn and fantasies as well. When we participate in any of these three areas, we create an imaginary world that centers on ourselves and where others are objects for our enjoyment. When we return to the real world, real people can't compete with our imaginary world. Not only this, but our ability to love in the real world is also weakened. Our habits of lust in our imaginary world become reality in our real love lives.

Lewis's thoughts are quite similar to what Jesus said in Matthew 5:27–28: "You have heard that it was said, 'You shall not commit adultery.' But I say to you that everyone who looks at a woman lustfully has already committed adultery with her in his heart."

Jesus doesn't pull any punches either. This is not because Jesus loves rules and gets a kick out of being strict; it is because Jesus knows the power of the mind and its ability to prevent us from truly loving others.

Sexual fantasies are thoughts that often lead to the actions and habits of masturbation and pornography. And masturbation and pornography can reinforce fantasies, which helps to create a very unhealthy cycle.

This maxim comes to mind: "Sow a thought, reap an action; sow an action, reap a habit; sow a habit, reap a character; sow a character, reap a destiny."

In light of this maxim, ask yourself: What do you want your character to be? What do you want your destiny to be? Do you want to be someone who can truly love others? If so, fantasies, masturbation, and pornography need to be addressed in your life. We will look at how to do this tomorrow.

Today's Detox Challenge

On a scale from 1 to 10 (10 being the highest), we would like you to rate yourself in two areas. First, where are you at when it comes to struggling with sexual fantasies, masturbation, and pornography? Second, if you are not in a good spot, how willing are you to change? Why or why not? Keep these numbers in mind as we head to tomorrow's chapter.

Day 20: Breaking Through

Yesterday's challenge was to help you identify just how much lust was a problem in your life and to help you gauge how willing you are to make necessary changes. Everything else in this chapter depends on your willingness to make those changes. God can't steer a parked car. We can't emphasize this enough. If you aren't convinced, then it won't happen.

We hope you do want to make changes or learn how to help others in their battle to fight sexual fantasies, masturbation, and pornography. Let's turn back to our stories about Xavier and Monica to learn how they were able to overcome their temptations.

Xavier

As you'll remember, Xavier began viewing porn in seventh grade. Throughout high school, he tried to give it up in fits and starts but with no meaningful results. Once it started affecting his dating relationships, he knew something had to change.

To begin, Xavier committed to praying the Rosary, frequenting Confession, and relying on the Eucharist. He told us, "When I got out of the habit of those things is when I would trip up."

Next, he did whatever he could not to be alone. "I'd go to the grocery store with my mom, just so I wouldn't be home alone. If I did get stuck there, I'd go for a run, even if I didn't need to. If I had already run that day and I was exhausted, I'd try to find a friend to be with."

Oh, and Xavier also did one more thing that helped: "I literally threw my laptop in the trash. I got to a point where I was so upset about my addiction that I knew I had to use the computer in the kitchen so I wouldn't be tempted."

All these things helped free Xavier from porn, which gave him a new freedom in dating. "In the past I wanted to use girls, now

I want to protect them. It was a complete change of view. To get to this point, all Christ had needed to work in my life was an open heart and some time."

Monica

Monica committed her life to Jesus and stepped up as a leader in her Catholic community, but she still struggled with masturbation, fantasies, and porn. She knew she needed to improve in these areas, but an additional urgency came about: "I realized that I wanted to work in full-time ministry and that I had to figure this out."

The summer before her senior year in college, Monica joined the Confraternity of the Angelic Warfare, a fellowship of men and women who commit themselves to pursuing and promoting chastity and frequenting Confession. Through her entire fall semester, she was able to avoid masturbating—until the last week of school. The stress of finals, along with living alone, caused her to fall again.

That winter, Monica attended a young adult conference and heard a "women only" talk on pornography and masturbation. The speaker helped her realize that many other women also struggle with these issues, not just her. As the speaker put it, "With men, it's like they share the same jail cell—they all know that they struggle with it. With women, it's like we're all in different cells!"

This revelation caused her to reach out to her girlfriends about her struggles. Soon an accountability group formed. She recounted, "If one of us was struggling we'd call each other on the phone or meet up if possible. This was our policy twenty-four hours a day, seven days a week."

Monica has come a long way with her addiction, but to this day she still has an accountability partner. When asked what advice she would have for other women, she said, "If you struggle with these temptations, learn to overcome the initial thoughts of 'I'm worthless' or 'I'm doomed never to figure out how to get out of it.' Bring your sins to light through Confession and then go from there."

Key Takeaways

Both Xavier's and Monica's stories bring out some great points that can be used if you battle with temptations in these areas. To help you gain the same freedom they have achieved, we've put together a list of key takeaways for you to consider:

Learn perseverance: As you saw in Xavier's and Monica's stories, getting over their addictions was not easy. They struggled for quite some time before they finally broke through. The key here is being convinced of what you need to do and finding new ways to fight back if you continue to struggle.

Use spiritual weapons: Both of them quickly ran to the Church seeking help and the grace to overcome temptation. Praying the Rosary, going to Eucharistic Adoration, and frequenting Confession, especially with the same priest, were key in helping them.

Form an accountability group: Monica and Xavier found people in their lives to help them out; they didn't try to wrestle with their struggles alone. Scripture tells us, "And though a man might prevail against one who is alone, two will withstand him. A threefold cord is not quickly broken" (Ecclesiastes 4:12). Find people who will truly hold you accountable. Establish creative ways of what to do when you struggle and what to do when you fall. For example,

Monica and a friend would text each other a fruit emoji if one of them was struggling and Monica would fast if one person in her accountability group fell.

Know yourself: Creating a habit of pornography and masturbation is not a result of chance. Many times there is a reason behind why we fall into these temptations. It's important to learn to know yourself. Why do you feel a need to take part in these things? What emptiness are you trying to fill? Why is that emptiness in your life?

Also, try to understand what triggers a fall. When temptation strikes, the acronym HALT—hungry, angry, lonely, tired—can be a useful tool to help you think about some of the reasons that might cause you to fall. By recognizing patterns, you can begin to find ways to break them and react differently so it doesn't happen again.

Don't be afraid to do something drastic: Neither Xavier nor Monica were afraid of taking drastic measures to remove these sins from their lives. Xavier was even willing to throw away his computer. Monica wasn't afraid to reach out to friends for help, even though she didn't yet know whether they struggled with the same thing.

Although we've done our best to come up with the most important takeaways, please do not think that this is an all-encompassing guide. Entire books and websites are dedicated to these topics, so this one chapter certainly can't cover everything. For an up-to-date list of the best resources out there, visit us at madetomagnify.com.

Today's Detox Challenge

Over the last two chapters, we hope you've been able to see what the sins of sexual fantasies, masturbation, and pornography really are, and to begin to understand what it's like to battle them.

Today's challenge is to develop an action plan for how you will overcome these temptations in your life. Visit theporneffect.com for everything you need to know to get started.

Day 21: Revealing

Men, this chapter may seem like it is only for women, but we think it's important for you to read it as well, so please don't skip it ... there is a challenge for you today, too!

As a Division 1 basketball player, Catherine spent a significant amount of time working out so that she was in top shape for her sport. Not only did all the exercise benefit her on the court, but it also gave her a body she was proud to highlight with the clothes she wore.

"I came from the perspective as an athlete that I worked hard for my body to look the way it did. My question was, 'Why would I hide my body?'"

When challenged about how her dress might affect men, she just shrugged her shoulders and said, "If a guy struggles with lust then it probably won't matter what I'm wearing. That's their issue ... it shouldn't dictate how I live my life or what I wear."

Catherine's perspective echoed that of many of the women I've spoken with on the topic of modesty. To them, the only reason you'd cover your body is if you were embarrassed by it; and if guys battled with objectifying women because of the way they dressed, well then, that was their problem.

Help a Brother Out

As you read in the last two chapters, difficulties with lusting after or fantasizing about others are real. You also know that the only one in charge of what another person does with his or her physical and emotional passions is *that person*. So, yes, in a sense, if the way a woman is dressed tempts a guy to lust, then it is his problem—but now that you know what a struggle it can be for guys to keep pure minds, would you be willing to do a few things to help a brother out?

Ladies, we're not asking you to be conscious of how your dress can affect men out of resentment or fear. Those are actually very dangerous reasons to dress modestly. Resenting guys because you think they can't control themselves can lead to an unhealthy opinion of them and their ability to choose to do the virtuous thing. Fearing that your body might cause a guy to stumble can lead to seeing your body as something that's bad and sinful when it's neither. If resentment and fear are your driving forces, then the chances of you truly embracing modesty with any semblance of joy will be low.

Rather, we're asking you to consider dressing modestly out of love—love for your brothers and a desire to do what you can to help them not to see you as a thing, but as a person who is an immortal daughter of the Most High King.

Change of Heart

Now, all of the above is good and true, and we hope you take it into consideration. But we've learned that it doesn't always speak to the *hearts* of women. Intellectually, sure, we get it, but sometimes we still don't care enough to make necessary changes.

If making changes in your life is only about others, then it's likely that you will be slower to act and will let the excuses flow. "I don't have money to buy modest clothing," "I dress much more modestly than other girls," and as Catherine said, "I work hard for my body," are all reasons interviewees gave us for why they put off dressing modestly. You have to see modesty not just as something you do for others but as something you do for yourself.

Modesty in dress is first and foremost a matter of the heart. Like chastity, if people are not convinced that developing the virtue of modesty is the best thing for others and for themselves, then a long list of objective reasons for being modest may not speak to them.

Too Little

So why dress modestly for yourself? Because immodest dress doesn't reveal too much; it reveals too little. It reveals too little of who you actually are. If the appearance of your body makes it hard for someone to look beyond your physically stimulating features, then it can distract from truly encountering the real you. And the real you is enough.

Do you know that? That who you are is enough? You don't need the world to tell you that you are beautiful to know that you are beautiful. You have been made in the image of a loving King and you are priceless. God doesn't make mistakes. He doesn't make junk. Your true beauty will never be discovered because your clothes highlight or reveal certain parts of your body. What will portray your true beauty can only come from within, so stop obsessing over trying to decorate a masterpiece.

P.S. Men, women need you to remind them that they are beautiful as they are. They need you to help them know their true worth and beauty so they don't go searching for it in ways that leave them feeling empty. You can honor them for their efforts when they strive to show you their true worth and beauty in the way they dress. The simple words "You look nice today" let them know they are on the right track.

Today's Detox Challenge

Today's challenge begins with a story.

When Anne was growing up she would always go shopping for new clothes with her mom. "We'd pick out lots of clothes and one by one I would try them on for her," Anne recounted. "After buying what we both liked, I would go home confident that I looked great and I was full of love and affirmation."

Although Anne looked and felt great, what she didn't consider when shopping with her mom was whether or not the clothes she had chosen were modest. As Anne began to understand that her dress was distracting others from truly encountering *her*, she decided that it was time to ask her heavenly mom what she thought.

"I looked in my closet and thought, 'What would my heavenly Mother Mary think of these clothes?' I went through my outfits one by one and imagined trying them on for her. What did *she* think? Did she like it? Did she want me to keep it? ... I got rid of many of my clothes that day and I continued to ask those questions for a while. Little by little, this changed the way I felt when I got dressed each day. Instead of thinking 'What will make me most attractive today?' and 'What will others think?' I began to ask, 'What will best express who I am today?' I began to choose clothing that drew people to see me for all that I was, body and soul."

Are there any articles of clothing in your closet that you would be uncomfortable trying on for Mary? For women, maybe it's a short dress, a low-cut top, a skintight garment, or an outfit that constantly requires you to adjust yourself. For men, maybe it's barely-there workout clothes, a T-shirt with graphics or words that don't convey your true worth and dignity, or clothes that are too skinny. Today we invite you to be bold and throw away at least one or two of these articles. Then when you get dressed tomorrow, ask yourself, "Would I wear this if I knew I was going to see Mary?" If you wouldn't, consider changing and getting rid of the clothes.

Discussion Questions for Week 3

1. For a culture that talks about sex so much, we rarely talk about its purpose. If you had to describe what our culture believes about the purpose of sex, what would you say?

2. What is God's teaching on the purpose of sexual intimacy? How could this change the way you approach a relationship?

3. We often think that chastity is about rules that restrict our freedom. How can God's plan for sex, dating, and relationships bring you freedom?

4. What's wrong with porn, masturbation, and sexual fantasies when it comes to living a life of authentic love?

5. What are some practical ways you've seen people be successful in overcoming porn, masturbation, and sexual fantasies?

6. How is your goal from Day 7 coming? Are you making any progress?

WEEK 4: EMOTIONAL PASSIONS

*Last week's focus was on the physical passions and our desire
for physical intimacy. You discovered that the purpose of sexual
intimacy is procreation and unity and that when we try to create
our own purpose for it, we end up disappointed because we are
violating its God-given nature. You also learned that in order for
love to be free of use it must reflect the love of the Trinity and be
free, faithful, total, and life-giving. You looked at the difference
between acts of affection and acts of arousal and saw how acts of
arousal, as well as sexual fantasies, pornography, masturbation,
even immodesty in our dress, violate God's vision for love.*

*Now that we have examined how our physical passions can either
lead us toward love or toward use, it is time to look at how our
emotional passions can do the same.*

Day 22: Two Types of Attractions

When I (Lisa) was just getting to know Kevin, two things struck
me about him. First, his intense blue eyes and chiseled face
instantly caught my attention. Second, I noticed that I really
enjoyed spending time with him. There was something about
his personality and charm that quickly made him one of my
favorite people.

Have you ever had this kind of experience? An experience when
you met someone and almost instantly found yourself drawn to
him or her? Although physically the person was a sight to behold,
your interest went beyond what your eyes perceived. There was
something deeper about the person that appealed to you.

What you felt in those moments are two distinct types of
attraction, physical attraction and emotional attraction.[1]

Physical and Emotional

Physical attractions are initiated by our physical passions. They have to do with what we find visibly attractive about a person on a *physical* level. This is the kind of attraction that made me think, "Kevin is handsome." When we are physically attracted to somebody we desire to encounter his or her body with the intention of drawing pleasure from the experience.

Emotional attractions are initiated by our emotional passions. Emotional attraction has to do with what we find attractive about a person in an invisible way at an *emotional* level. This is the kind of attraction that made me think, "Kevin is charming." When we are emotionally attracted to somebody we desire to encounter the invisible attributes of a person with the intention of drawing pleasure from the experience.

Oftentimes when we set out to get things right in the realm of love, dating, and sex, we tend to focus solely on the struggles that can arise from our physical attractions and passions. If we can just kick our porn addiction, stop hooking up, control our sexual fantasies, and no longer lust after others, then it will be smooth sailing, right? While these are great and necessary steps toward being free to love and be loved, they do not take into consideration the struggles that can arise from our emotional attractions and passions, too.

The Job of the Emotions

Before we begin, let's get one thing straight: an emotional connection is healthy and necessary for any romantic relationship. God did not create us to be robots that are devoid of feelings and emotion. As a married woman, if I told my husband that I have no intention of ever leaving him but that my feelings for him were now no stronger than the feelings that I have for a pile of rocks, he rightfully would be distraught.

God delights in the emotional love that is shared between couples, and he uses it as a powerful agent in bringing them closer together and unifying them. In the lifelong commitment of marriage, an emotional bond provides a couple with a way to remain close to one another even if they are physically far apart. This bond is essential for getting couples through difficult times that test their ability to remain faithful to each other in the fullest sense of the word.

Emotional attraction also plays an important role in making it possible for authentic love to begin and grow. Years ago, the initial spark of attraction opened my (Lisa's) heart to the possibility of forming what is now my vocation in marriage. I cherish the memory of my inability to eat for three days after Kevin asked me out on our first date. I smile when I remember the feeling of sitting across from him at Lidia's Restaurant and thinking, "Is this really happening? Am I seriously on a date with Kevin Cotter?" I treasure all the beautiful emotions that came with our love story and the ones that continue to arise from our marriage today.

Emotions Alone Do Not Equal Love

The emotions are an essential component of authentic love, but we must be careful not to confuse feelings with love itself. This can be very difficult to grasp in our world today, which speaks of emotional highs as the defining factor of true love. We are told that love is present if there are butterflies and fireworks and that if one day there are not, well then, the love must be gone—it's time to move on.

Authentic love, however, goes much deeper than the spontaneous emotional reactions of heart-stopping moments. It is a conscious choice to will the good of another. This does not mean that authentic love is void of emotion, but rather that it is properly led by the intellect and integrates the passion-led emotions into love as a whole.

Remember, we're not suggesting that you become cold creatures who look at everything through the lenses of calculated reason and seek to suppress any and all emotion. To desire emotional satisfaction or to derive pleasure from a shared emotional experience are not bad things. These are legitimate human needs. But we must remember that the emotions are part of our *passions* and, if the passions are not properly directed by the will and the intellect, then instead of leading us toward happiness, they can lead us away from it.

P.S. Guys, I (Kevin) want to remind you that this week isn't just for the ladies. We have emotions, too. We might not always show them as strongly or understand them as well, but this doesn't mean that we don't have them or that they don't affect us. In fact, because guys don't often talk about their feelings, you might actually learn more than the opposite sex during this week. And you'll understand women a lot better, too. Don't be afraid to dive in.

Today's Detox Challenge

When we met with Carlos, whose story was told on Day 11, he told us that one of the first steps he took in turning around his life as a stripper was running to Jesus's mother, Mary, for her support. Knowing that his heart was so broken and twisted, on his twentieth birthday Carlos asked Our Lady of Guadalupe for a new one. By entrusting his heart to his Mother in Heaven, Carlos felt confident that she would share his needs, including the ones he didn't know he had, with her Son. As we begin this week that deals with matters of the heart, we challenge you to invite Mary into your heart.

Mary knows Jesus better than anyone else. When we ask her to share our needs with her Son, she does so in a way that only a mother can. You can always share your struggles and needs with Mary and ask her to present them to Jesus for you. After all, what loving son can refuse the eager requests of his mother?

Day 23: Projectors

Some of my (Lisa's) fondest memories of my dad, who I am sure has been partying in Heaven since he passed away when I was in college, are of dancing with him. He was a great dancer, and as a kid I loved having him twirl me around on the dance floor. Thanks to many, many wonderful father-daughter dances and wedding receptions, one of my secret desires was to marry a man who could whisk me around like my dad did.

When Kevin and I first became friends we were working together as counselors at a summer camp. On the last night of each camp session, the final hurrah was a party that consisted of eating ice cream sundaes and dancing. During this time I had the chance to cut a rug on the dance floor with my fellow counselors, including Kevin. I was already admiring him from afar, and he stood out as a great dancer.

When we first started dating I was excited for any opportunity we had to share our mutual love of dancing, but slowly I started to notice that something was off. Kevin's dancing ability was waning, as if he was losing his rhythm. The longer we were together, the more awkward he became on the dance floor. By the time we were married, it was completely gone. It was then that I realized that his ability to dance didn't decline with time; it was never really there to begin with.

Running with It

In my desire to marry someone who could dance with me, I projected the quality of being a good dancer onto Kevin. I decided that his signature fist pumps and spin moves from our camp days proved that he would be able to twirl me around on the dance floor, but that was not the case.

What I did with Kevin and his dancing ability is something we do to the people we are attracted to all the time. We desire a certain quality in a person and when we find a glimmer of that quality, we run with it. You've done this. We know you have because Pope St. John Paul II told us so.

"In the eyes of a person sentimentally committed to another person the value of the beloved object grows enormously—as a rule out of all proportion to his or her real value." [2]

What Pope St. John Paul II means is that when we like someone, we search for what we want him or her to be and we tend to find it. Not necessarily because that quality or characteristic exists but because we want it to.

When it comes to the small things, the consequences are small, and they can be cause for a good laugh. (Trust me, we laugh about my dreams of Kevin and me captivating everyone at wedding receptions.) However, when it comes to the big things, the consequences are much greater.

Back to Jack

Remember my boyfriend Jack from Day 9? The guy who made me canned soup for Valentine's Day and then broke up with me because I wouldn't sleep with him? Yep, that Jack—well, he was definitely a guy I projected a few important qualities onto.

When it came to dating, I had a few non-negotiable items on my list of what I was looking for in a boyfriend. At the top of the list were these two: he should be a guy who is striving for holiness, and a guy who would support my decision to save sex for marriage.

Jack and I never really talked about our faith, but since he attended a Catholic high school, and sometimes we would go to Mass together on Sunday, I took these small facts and blew them out of proportion. I created my own opinion about Jack's holiness, basically affirming that he was St. Joseph.

When it came to saving sex for marriage, early on in our relationship I told Jack about my commitment to wait. He sat there silently and listened to me as I fumbled through my explanation. When I was done he had no comments on the topic, and we quickly moved on to something else. Despite the fact that Jack was not a virgin, I took his silence as consent and concluded that he was the best boyfriend ever, that he loved me enough to respect my decision to save sex for marriage, and that he would never pressure me to change my mind.

Blinded

In my mind, my two most important criteria had been met and Jack passed the "good boyfriend" test with flying colors. Check and check, right? Actually, no. I wanted Jack to pass the test because I wanted to have a boyfriend. So I projected qualities onto him that he didn't actually have. Rather than letting my will and intellect weigh in on the reality of these important factors, I allowed my emotions to lead the charge and they got it wrong.

The red flags that pointed to the truth about Jack were there; I just didn't want to acknowledge them. My emotional passions desired to be in a relationship. I loved the feeling of being called "babe" and "sweetheart." I loved having a hand to hold and a date on Friday night. I loved being able to tell others that I had a boyfriend because it made me feel important. I wanted it all so badly that I allowed myself to be blinded about the truth of who Jack really was. I made excuses for the red flags and acted as if everything was great! I wanted to love and be loved, but my approach made it difficult for me to see the reality of our relationship clearly and where it was ultimately headed.

Be Aware

The ways in which you will exaggerate and project qualities onto people you are attracted to is a tendency you need to be fully aware of. Remember, as a rule, we will do this, so it can't be avoided. (Trust us, this is not just a women's issue. We've seen plenty of guys project all sorts of things onto a woman just because she's unbelievably gorgeous.)

However, you can consciously work to allow your intellect to engage in this process by asking Pope St. John Paul II's question: "Is it really so?"[3] Are the qualities, virtues, and values that I see in this person real, or am I projecting my own desires on to this person? Actively engaging your intellect in this way will help you to avoid being unpleasantly surprised in the future.

Today's Detox Challenge

In today's chapter Lisa talked about her list of non-negotiable characteristics that she wanted in a person in order to enter into a relationship. Included on the list were things such as striving for holiness, supporting her decision to save sex for marriage (although it should have been *wanting* to save sex for marriage himself), honesty, trustworthiness, and so on.

Today we'd like you to consider taking out your journal and writing "Is it really so?" at the top of a new page. Below that title begin a list of your non-negotiable items. Then, the next time you are considering entering into a relationship with somebody, read each item on your list and ask, "Is it really so?" Does this person truly meet these criteria or not? If you are unsure about some of the items, then we suggest you wait until you get to know them better before you enter into a relationship. If the person does not really meet your criteria, then be courageous and trust that God desires something better for you.

Day 24: The Fake Happy World

When Brandon started coming over to hang out at Samantha's dorm at regular intervals, she assumed it could mean only one thing: he liked her. Between the back massages, long hugs, and Brandon calling her his best friend, she was certain that she hadn't gotten it wrong. So when Brandon asked out Samantha's roommate, Maggie, she was shocked.

Samantha explained, "I tried to convince myself that I didn't really like him and that everything was fine, but inside it was completely killing me. It was so bad."

Despite her mental pep talks, Samantha couldn't get past her feelings for Brandon. She found herself spending hours daydreaming about him, obsessively checking his social media feeds, rearranging her schedule so that she might see him, and still hoping that they might one day have a future together.

"I think I did those things because it gave me a sense of purpose," recalled Samantha. "It sounds shallow, but I felt like I needed to like someone, I needed something to occupy my time … I was longing to be loved."

This longing for love was so deep in Samantha's heart that she found herself grasping at ways to feel loved by Brandon in any form she could get. "There was this one time when I was with Brandon and I was imagining that he was my boyfriend. In that moment I can remember specifically thinking, 'This feels so good, so I'm just going to keep going with it. I know it's not reality, but it's the only thing I have, so it'll have to be good enough for now.'"

Grasping

Have you ever been there? Grasping for emotional fulfillment in any way you can get it, even though you know that what you are experiencing is not real?

Maybe you grasp for it by mentally stalking someone as you imagine your future together. Maybe you grasp for it in a friendship that you have allowed to turn into a fake "something more" that exists only in your mind. Maybe you grasp for it by creeping on someone's social media accounts so you can feel like you are interacting with the person and getting to know Mr. or Miss Wonderful.

In whatever form it takes, when you grasp for love, what you are really doing is escaping into your fake "happy" world because your real one isn't working out.

The Fake Happy World

In our fake happy world, our emotional desires can be met temporarily and it feels good. Since it is controlled entirely by our own thoughts and imagination, we can enter into it whenever we please. It's a magical place that doesn't depend on the cooperation of others, requires no commitments, and expects nothing from us.

At first glance it sounds good, but living in the fake happy world can lead to a lot of misery, especially if it never becomes a reality. This is exactly what happened to Samantha.

One Taco

After Brandon and Maggie broke up, Samantha knew it was time to tell Brandon how she truly felt about him. Unfortunately, the only emotion he showed during the conversation was shock.

"For weeks afterward I couldn't sleep or eat," Samantha told us. "I always thought girls who did this were ridiculous, but there I was. ... During my hour lunch break at work I'd force myself to eat one taco from Taco Bell, then I'd go home and lie on the floor and think, 'Okay, you have forty-five minutes to cry,' all over a boy who never said he liked me. There was never anything between us except for how I had let things go so far in my mind."

Samantha felt like she was going through a breakup even though no real relationship ever existed between her and Brandon.

So what went wrong? How did it get to that point? Well, in short, Samantha tried to use Brandon for emotional fulfillment, but it never worked. It couldn't work. It always left her wanting more because her fake happy world was not based on authentic love, it was based on use.

Let us point out here that Samantha is not a crazy ball of irrational emotions. For the ladies reading this, you are probably shaking your heads in sympathy. For the men, you might be thinking, "No? Seriously? Is this for real?" Yes, it is for real, and no, Samantha and the rest of the female population are not crazy. It is all just part of how emotional passions can mess with women … and how they can mess with men too.

Use

You've already learned that people are not things to be used. Their worth and value as people with immortal souls is too great. It can be easy to see how physically or emotionally using a boyfriend or girlfriend, or sexually fantasizing about someone, turns a person into an object for use. But it can be harder to see how emotionally fantasizing about someone can do the same.

When we grasp at emotional pleasure by entering into the fake happy world, we are allowing ourselves to fantasize emotionally. It is good, healthy, and normal to have hopes and dreams about the future. Daydreaming about what life might be like one day is nothing to be concerned about, but if our daydreams are pointed at a particular person in the hopes of gaining some sort of temporary pleasure from the experience, they begin to turn into use.

At first glance, activities such as mental stalking and social media creeping can seem harmless because just thinking about someone can't hurt. Heck, the person doesn't even have to know about it. *Sounds a lot like the lines we use to justify sexual fantasies, doesn't it?*

Just as sexual fantasies objectify a person, emotional fantasies do the same. When we enter into our fake happy world, we turn the person into an object, using him or her for the emotional high we get from our imaginary relationship. It's use because the person is not the recipient of our affection. The person has become a means, or a tool, that we are using to get one-sided, counterfeit emotional pleasure. Using another person as an object from which to gain pleasure is always in direct contrast with authentic love, no matter which form it is in.

P.S. If you are wondering if this is something that only women do, let me (Kevin) assure you, it's not. We spoke with several guys who struggled with grasping at emotional fulfillment. Just to name one, there was Corey, who told us about his forty-women long "potential wives list." With that list, Corey would escape into a world where he imagined what a future with each candidate might look like. It wasn't until a friend challenged him to burn his list that he was able to surrender his future to Christ and begin to see women as sisters in Christ, not as objects to use for emotional pleasure.

Today's Detox Challenge

When you find yourself escaping into your fake happy world to use someone emotionally, we challenge you to train your brain to stop. As soon as you notice yourself trying to grasp at a fake feeling of love, replace those thoughts with a prayer mantra. It can be the words of the first Christians, such as, "My Lord and my God!" (John 20:28), "Lord, if you will, you can make me clean" (Matthew 8:2), or "Jesus, son of David, have mercy on me!" (Luke 18:38). It can be a prayer asking for the intercession of your patron saint or our Mother Mary. Whatever it is, keep it short and memorable. Jot down your mantra in your journal and commit it to memory, so you can recall it and continually repeat it until the temptation has passed.

HAIL MARY
FULL OF GRACE,
KICK THE
DEVIL IN THE
FACE

Day 25: The Holy of Holies

In a letter to the people of Corinth, St. Paul wrote to the faithful, "Do you not know that your body is a temple of the Holy Spirit within you, which you have from God? You are not your own; you were bought with a price. So glorify God in your body" (1 Corinthians 6:19–20). We've always loved this analogy, which points to the truth that the very Spirit of God is housed in each and every one of us. For this reason, we have to be careful with the way we use our bodies, so as to not defile their sacredness.

The actual Temple of Jesus's time would have been a wondrous sight to see. It was enormous, mighty, complex, and constantly bustling with people, as it was the center of Jewish culture and religion. The building itself was divided into many layers of courts. As you traveled deeper into the Temple, each court became more and more exclusive, with fewer people being allowed to enter. At the center of the Temple, you would find the Holy of Holies, where God dwelled. This most sacred of spaces was guarded by a veil, and throughout the history of the Temple few people were ever permitted to go behind it.

Our Heart of Hearts

If we take this analogy of our bodies as temples of the Holy Spirit one step further, we can relate the innermost depths of our heart of hearts to the Holy of Holies. It is here in the depths of our heart that our hopes, dreams, longings, and sincere prayers reside. This is also the place where our scars, secrets, fears, and disappointments lie. At times it can be a place of refuge filled with happy memories, and on other occasions it can be a place of torment as we recall painful and depressing events. This most intimate place that houses our deepest emotions and life-altering memories is the place in our heart where we long to be understood by others and ourselves.

Our desire to know ourselves and be known by others is a good and natural desire given to us by God. However, there can be a danger in how this desire manifests itself if, rather than making mindful decisions that have been directed by our intellect, we allow our emotions to run the show.

Pulling Back the Veil

In our longing to be understood, it can become a real temptation to pull back the veil that protects our heart of hearts and invite someone, and on occasion just anyone, into this sacred place in an attempt to help make sense of the mess we may find there. Sometimes we can be so desperate to be understood that we are willing to expose ourselves to people who may not have proven themselves worthy of being in such an intimate place.

As we search for acceptance of who we are, as we are, we can begin to grasp for love by sharing our hopes, fears, scars, and desires with unworthy people. It's our attempt to fill our deep-seated craving to find the solutions, relief, and understanding we long for. In this process, we find emotional intensity and attachment increasing as we bare our soul to this person. We begin to believe this person will always be there for us and never leave because we've been through so much together. But if the relationship ends, then it won't feel quite right because what the person knows about us can't become "un-known." A part of our heart of hearts has been given away and we cannot take it back.

It Doesn't Feel Sacred Anymore

How many of us have allowed ourselves to cycle through this process over and over again, only to find that our heart of hearts doesn't feel sacred anymore? When we admit that various people know deeply personal things about our lives, yet we still feel as confused and broken as ever, we can be tempted to build walls and harden our hearts to those around us.

If this happens, we can go from one extreme of grasping for love to the opposite extreme of pushing love away. This pushing away can come in the form of ignoring, talking back to, giving the silent treatment to, or intentionally withholding affection from the people we love. It's done in the hope that vigilant protection of our hearts means not getting hurt, but in the end it leaves us shut out from life and love.

God doesn't want us to be lonely and isolated. We were made to love and be loved. We were made to live in relationship with one another. But if we do not learn to guard our hearts with the same respect as we guard our bodies, we can end up bitter, disappointed, and broken.

Today's Detox Challenge

Today's challenge requires you to pull out the list of triggers that you created on Day 5. The things that can lead to physical regrets are often the same things that can lead to emotional ones. We suggest you ask yourself if there is anything that should be added to this list, such as late-night phone conversations, alcohol, lack of sleep, or prolonged isolation. These are all things that might set you up for sharing what you will one day wish you could take back.

If looking at this list reveals that you have fallen into your old habits, don't give up on yourself. Now is as good a time as any to recommit to living the new standards that will help lead you to be truly free to love and be loved. Today is a new day. You can do this.

Day 26: Where Our Hearts Go...

As a freshman in college, Teagan was thrilled to gain the attention of a handsome upperclassman named Will. Having never been in a real relationship before, she found everything about the experience exhilarating. His admiring glances from across the room, her heart stopping when he called, the anticipation of the next time they'd see each other—she soaked it all in with great pleasure.

Within a few weeks of meeting, Will officially became Teagan's first boyfriend and, much to her surprise, their relationship began to progress rapidly.

"I got emotionally attached to him really quickly," she explained. "Soon I felt like if we were going to be serious, then I should tell him everything about me. I felt obligated to share."

That is just what Teagan did. She shared everything about her scars from the past. She shared the details of her current struggles. She shared the moments in her life that shaped her into who she is, and all the while her attachment to Will increased.

"Entrusting things to him, and his being so gentle in responding to them, it made me feel secure. He was gentle with me in ways that I wasn't gentle with myself, so I started to run to him for security."

Teagan liked the haven she found in Will. As she gave him intimate access to her heart, he gave her the security she had always longed for. For the first time in her life, Teagan felt that she truly mattered to somebody.

With Will being so generous in providing her with the things she desired, Teagan found herself wanting to do the same for him. Will's desires, however, were not only for emotional gratification; but deep down, what Will also desired was access to Teagan's body for physical gratification.

"I was surprised at how quickly we became tempted to be unchaste," Teagan recalled thoughtfully. "When it came to physical stuff, I didn't want to disappoint him."

She had entrusted her heart to Will, and when he accepted her as she was, she was surprised that despite her hesitations she felt drawn to entrust her body to him as well.

Following

Our physical and emotional passions are so interconnected that they cannot help but want to speak the same language. If our emotions are saying, "I love this person, something in me wants us to be as close as possible, and I can't help but want to share everything," then our bodies will also want to say, "I love this person, something in me wants us to be as close as possible, and I can't help but want to share ... *everything*."

If there is only one thing you remember from this week, then we want you to remember this: *where our hearts go, our bodies will want to follow.*

In its proper place (marriage), this kind of deeply unified love is a beautiful thing. After all, the purpose and outcomes of sexual intimacy are physical (babies) and emotional (bonding). It's all part of God's design. However, outside of marriage, as was the case with Teagan and Will, broken hearts, guilty regrets, and disappointment can follow.

The Impossible Blueprint

Having a proper emotional depth in a relationship is vital, not only for couples to protect each other's hearts, but also to protect each other's bodies. However, defining how close is too close in black-and-white terms is impossible. We wish we could give you an easy-to-follow guide for when to share what information, but the human heart is just not that simple.

We each have different personalities and temperaments that handle emotional data and experiences in a variety of ways. We each have different scars and wounds that are in various stages of acceptance and healing. We each have different strengths and struggles that create a myriad of needs for navigating our emotions with virtue. When you combine all these factors and multiply the complexity by two people, it is impossible to give a clear path for the pace at which a couple should go about sharing their hearts and growing in emotional intimacy.

Despite the complexity of the situation, it is vital for couples to increase the emotional depth of their relationships over time, so we don't want to leave you completely empty-handed. Below are a few general guidelines you can turn to as you develop the skills and virtues (such as prudence!) needed to navigate this essential part of authentic relationships, without letting it lead to physical or emotional regret.

Take it to prayer: This is the best advice we can give you on this topic. Pray about it. Pray for wisdom to know what to share and when to share it. Invite God into the process and ask the Holy Spirit to guide you.

Seek counsel: Having an outside perspective on matters of the heart can help you see clearly. Talk through your desires and concerns with your accountability partner, a trusted mentor, family member, or spiritual director who can help you discern whether you are on the right path.

Check your motivation: If you find yourself desiring to share something that's going on in your heart, then it's helpful to examine your motive. Why do you want to share this particular thing? Are you seeking unhealthy attention? Are you hoping that by sharing you'll receive the emotional affirmation that you long for? Are you in search of an emotional high? Or is your longing to share based upon a desire to grow as a couple in a manner that is proper to the current state of your relationship?

Spare the details: Having conversations that begin, "How far have you gone?" or "What's the worst thing that's ever happened to you?" serve mainly to satisfy idle curiosity and can stir up unnecessary images and desires. You don't owe your boyfriend or girlfriend a detailed account of your sexual history and deepest scars. There may come a time when general information about events that will affect your relationship needs to be shared, but spare the details.

When it's right, be vulnerable: The loving exchange of accepting and being accepted is a beautiful expression of God's endless mercy, love, and acceptance of us. In any relationship there will come times when a couple needs to admit their weaknesses, share certain scars, and be vulnerable with one another. When those times come, if you cannot give or accept that depth of vulnerability, then it is important to ask yourself why.

Oftentimes this reluctance is due to a wound that you carry from trusting the wrong people in the past. But if someone is truly worthy of your trust, then you need to honor that person by offering it. Be open and honest about why you have hesitations and ask the Lord to begin the process of healing your wounds so you can experience the depth of love that he desires you to live.

Finally, we want to point out that it's one thing for a couple to mutually support each other's emotional needs; it's another thing for one party to carry the weight of another's emotional needs. If you find yourself feeling constantly burned out or like you need to motivate yourself mentally to keep investing in a relationship, then these may be signs that something is not right in your relationship. If this is you, take your concerns to both

Jesus in prayer and to a trusted friend or mentor who can help you sort out what is appropriate or inappropriate.

Today's Detox Challenge

Your desire for emotional fulfillment is a legitimate need. Have you ever thought about how you go about meeting it? In your journal, we invite you to write down a list of ways that you seek out emotional fulfillment, both positive and negative. Then, find time today to engage in one of the positive ways that you meet your emotional needs.

Day 27: You Don't Need a Savior

Yesterday we began the story of Teagan, whose body followed her heart in giving too much too soon to her boyfriend Will. Today there's more to her story.

Two years after Teagan and Will began dating, Teagan started to listen intently to the patient knocking of Jesus on her heart's door. As she became more and more convinced that true happiness would only come from pursuing a relationship with Jesus and his Church, she was torn. She understood that she was breaking God's rules, yet she was so attached to Will that she couldn't imagine breaking up.

The only thing Teagan could think to do was pray. She began to beg God to help her and Will set things straight in their relationship, and in his mercy, God answered. By seeing Teagan come alive in her faith, Will's heart began to open up to the call to greatness that God had planned for him as well. Together they were able to commit to pursuing chastity in an authentically pure relationship.

Wanted to Feel Wanted

Despite their successes, Teagan's heart was still heavy from the mistakes they had made.

"Even though we weren't being physical anymore, I felt an overwhelming amount of guilt and shame about the past. A wall was up in my prayer time," shared Teagan, as she struggled to find the right words. She explained how one day, while sitting in a chapel, her heart was so laden with guilt that she couldn't take it anymore. "Okay, Jesus, I really don't want to talk about this," she pleaded. "I was annoyed that I had to face what had happened," Teagan explained to us. "I couldn't understand why I let myself get into this."

While Teagan sat in the chapel soaking in her confusion, a thought suddenly came to her: "*You did it because you wanted to feel wanted.*"

There it was.

Teagan finally admitted it.

She had given intimate parts of her heart and body to try to fill an aching void that desperately wanted to feel wanted.

As she allowed the hard truth to flood over her, God's voice reached out and tenderly whispered, "*Well, I want you.*"

"It was so spontaneous and clear that it couldn't have been anything else," said Teagan sincerely. "I cried as I let the truth of that sink in. … I didn't even know that the God of the universe wanted me, so I had to go looking in all these other places, when all along *he wanted me.*"

God wants you. Even when you feel like nobody else does. He. Wants. You. Do you know that? In the depths of your heart, do you truly know that *he wants you*?

Searching

If you don't know that the God of the universe wants you, it is easy to go searching for that affirmation in others. It can be easy to think that if you just had a boyfriend or a girlfriend who wanted you, then you would be satisfied and the void that you feel in your life would be filled. But the truth is that no matter how wonderful or holy boyfriends or girlfriends can be, they will never be able to fill that void. It's just not their job.

What Teagan desired from Will was something that he fundamentally could never give her. She wanted him to be the one to affirm her value, give her security in an unpredictable world, show her that she mattered, define her worth, and prove to her that she was wanted. What Teagan wanted was for Will to be her *savior*.

At first it seemed like her plan was working. As she gave pieces of her heart and body to him it made her feel wanted, but the high eventually wore off and to bring it back again she had to give even more. It was a cycle that Teagan couldn't understand until she finally discovered that day in the chapel that her plan would never have worked. She actually didn't need Will to be her savior. She already had one.

Unlocking the Mystery

If you want to unlock the mystery behind why so many relationships end in regret and heartache, understanding that a person cannot be your savior is the key. When our desires to love and be loved are painfully unfulfilled, it can lead to using others physically or emotionally. Usually we're not trying to be selfish and intentionally use people—we're just so desperately hungry that we don't know what else to do. But as we've unpacked over these last few weeks, this kind of behavior can never lead to lasting happiness. It actually leaves us emptier than ever.

In your brokenness and emptiness, the only thing that can truly satisfy is Jesus. He loves you. He's proud of you. He wants to fill the void in your life that only he can fill. Let him be your savior and your life will never be the same.

Today's Detox Challenge

You don't need a savior because you already have one. That Savior is here, and you can go see him anytime you want in the tabernacle or in the Eucharistic Adoration chapel at your nearest church. Have you visited him lately? Today's challenge is to pull out your calendar right now, find your next available hour, and go see Jesus. Spend some time with the one who loves you more than any other person can or will. Sit in his presence and just *be* with him. As interviewee Therese beautifully put it, "Once I knew that Jesus gave me his Body in the Eucharist, I stopped feeling the need to search for anyone else's."

Day 28: Besties

I (Kevin) began striving to live my life for Jesus at a fairly early age. During the summer between eighth grade and high school, my brother encouraged me to join a Bible study at our local youth group. Slowly over the course of the summer, I began to understand what it meant for Jesus to die for me, and everything changed.

After my conversion, I had to face some practical questions. Who was I supposed to hang out with on the weekend? Would it be possible to find anyone who shared my commitment to Jesus?

As I looked around during the first few weeks of high school, I didn't have much hope. But as I stayed committed to my faith, I slowly began to discover new friends, and we started to form a band of brothers.

Proverbs 17:17 says, "A friend loves at all times, and a brother is born for adversity." High school was filled with adversity, but with my band of brothers I was better equipped to face the challenges. If we were struggling with an area of lust, we would call each other to something higher. If a problem arose in our lives, we were there for advice. If one of us came under attack, we knew our brothers had our back.

People in high school began to identify us as a group, rather than as individuals. We encouraged one another and drew strength from each other. These friendships helped us not only to avoid temptations, but also to grow in our faith and live the lives that we felt God truly calling us to. I know my faith, both in high school and today, would have been much different without my band of brothers.

Don't Go It Alone

In all the interviews we conducted for this book, there were always two big factors that helped people not to use others emotionally—Jesus and a community of friends who love him.

Through Teagan's story we spent a lot of time looking at the importance of Jesus. Now we want to look at the importance of having friends who love him.

Ultimately Jesus is the only one who can fulfill your fundamental desires for love, worth, and security. However, he never intended for you to spend your life on earth alone and emotionally isolated from other humans. He gave us friends to help us to grow in holiness and challenge us to become who we are truly created to be. He also gave us friends so we can meet the legitimate needs of our emotional passions in a healthy way. When we are engaged in a community that loves and supports us, we are less likely to run to romantic relationships in an unhealthy attempt to fill an emotional void.

We have found this to be especially true when it comes to same-sex friends. No, we're not telling you that you can't have opposite-sex friends; rather, we want to highlight the importance of having friends who can understand you as only a fellow man or woman can.

Here's why it matters. First, if you become emotionally intimate with the opposite sex, the risk of at least one party eventually desiring to be more than friends increases, which can lead to awkwardness if the feelings aren't returned. Second, someone from the opposite sex may be able to tell you when you are not being a good man or woman, but not *how* to be a man or woman.

Band of Brothers

Men, I (Kevin) once heard a college chaplain talk about how guys experience the beginning of manhood:

"It begins in the fifth grade as hormones emerge. From this time, guys can feel out of control, ashamed, and confused. They joke about manhood, brag about it, laugh about it, read about it, Google it ... all of these efforts are attempts to figure out their masculinity because they don't feel like they are in control."

From the moment of puberty, guys are trying to figure out manhood. We try to learn about it from books, the Internet, women ... basically anything that might give us a clue. This is the part where learning about masculinity from other men comes in.

Just like the friends I had in high school, men need other men who get them: men who understand the struggles of lust, but strive to live the freedom that Christ gives; men who are aware of the costs of sacrificing their lives for the Lord and others, but don't let that stop them from doing it anyway; men who are willing to share their wounds and scars that they've experienced as men, but still choose hope. A band of brothers can help men be men through dedication, challenges, and perseverance.

Squad of Sisters

Ladies, I (Lisa) am sure each of you reading this has at least one scar from female relationships in the past. Gossiping, backstabbing, and guy drama can all be accomplished in one Friday night in our world. It can seem like befriending only guys would make life easier. This might work in the short term, but for the long haul? You've got to admit: we need each other.

Only fellow sisters can fully understand the need for fat pants, the logic of crying for no real reason, the healing power of chocolate, and why sometimes going to the store in the middle of the night for Tylenol is necessary. Only sisters can fully understand your superior ability to mentally stalk a guy with precision and detail. Only sisters can help you figure out what authentic femininity looks like in today's time and culture.

I know it takes courage to trust another woman when you have been hurt before, but you can't go it alone when it comes to this whole womanhood thing. You will need your sisters to pick you up when you are struggling on this journey. Start praying for the courage to let them in.

Where Are They?

Finding a band of brothers or a squad of sisters to call your own can be a challenge. If you don't have one already, then you might look around and wonder, "Where are these amazing people hiding?" They are out there, but finding them may push you out of your comfort zone.

The easiest place to begin is your own church or Catholic campus center. Is there a youth group or young adult group you could check out? Also, think about your own acquaintances. Do you already know some people who are striving to live for Christ? Start hanging out with them and ask them to introduce you to some of their friends who love Jesus. Keep praying for opportunities to develop strong same-sex friendships, and God will either bring you friends or bring you peace as you wait.

Today's Detox Challenge

Today we challenge you to plan a girls' or guys' night with your friends who love Jesus. Sometime over the next week gather together with those who are striving to live authentic masculinity or femininity. Let that time strengthen your emotional life so you don't turn to using others to fill a void.

Discussion Questions for Week 4

1. What role does attraction play in relationships? How can we use attraction for the sake of love instead of lust?

2. Have you ever been in a relationship where love made you blind to someone's weaknesses or faults? How so?

3. What practical steps can you take to keep your emotions in check so you don't make these mistakes again?

4. The book discussed how emotional fulfillment is a legitimate need. What are some ways that you can fulfill it in a proper way?

5. Have you ever experienced a band of brothers or a squad of sisters before? How can a strong group of friends shape your ability to love authentically?

6. It can be so easy to find our fulfillment in relationships instead of in the Lord. What are some ways you can remind yourself that your relationship with the Lord comes first?

Week 5: Dating

Last week's focus was on the ways our emotional passions can lead us to use others. We looked at how projecting desired attributes onto others, escaping into the fake happy world, desperately letting people into the holy of holies, and expecting others to be our savior are just some of the emotional pitfalls that will prevent us from giving and receiving authentic love. However, if we can learn to allow our intellects and wills to direct our emotional passions, they can become properly integrated into our relationships in ways that lead to authentic love.

This week we are shifting away from the topics of passions and use to begin focusing on dating. We will look at how to determine if a person may be right for you and where to go from there. But first, we have one more thought on friends.

Day 29: Old Friends

Joining a fraternity his freshmen year of college seemed to be the natural thing for Sam to do. After all, he had already been living the stereotypical "frat life" while in high school, so why not extend it into college?

Life was cruising along for Sam until one night, while setting up for a party, Jesus allowed him to see the emptiness of the life he was pursuing. In the midst of lining up kegs and chasers, Jesus said to Sam, "What are you doing? This isn't how I taught you to live or who I called you to be." Not being able to deny the call he had just received, he walked out of the party in a daze.

After this powerful experience, Sam knew his life could never be the same. With initiation into the fraternity just around the corner, he had to ask, "Should I go through with it, or get out?" For Sam, there was no real choice. He looked around at his fraternity brothers and saw in them the same emptiness that he had finally found the remedy for. More than anything he wanted to share with them the peace that he knew was possible, and what better way to do it than by walking side by side with them and pointing them to Christ?

Here's what Sam decided: "When it came time to initiate, I stood in front of my pledge brothers and told them I'd no longer be drinking with them, but that I'd be there for them. They were all really upset because that's how they'd come to know me. They were also skeptical and tested it and tried to get me to go back, but I stood up to them and said, 'No. This is not what I want. If you are my friends, you'll respect my decisions.' Given time, they did."

Being a Light

With the changes that were going on in Sam's life, he found himself naturally drawn to his campus Newman Center. The men there called him to be holier and strive for sanctity, which is exactly what he needed in order to be a witness of Christ's love to his fraternity brothers.

Sam explained, "I knew that God had called me to be a light in the dark lives of my brothers, but I wouldn't have been able to do it without the support of my brothers in Christ. The men I met at the Newman Center showed me how to live life well and how to live authentically. I brought this life into my fraternity and it really changed the way in which I approached my friendships with my fraternity brothers. They became deeper and we had more meaningful discussions about life, God, women ... I started a Bible study in the fraternity, and a lot of my brothers started to come to Mass with me and desired to better their lives as well by surrounding themselves with good people. They saw what had happened to me and wanted it themselves."

Old Friends

For some of you, being on this journey will make you want to run from your "old friends," but that's not really what we want you to do. (Unless there are circumstances in which you know you need to cut ties completely with a group of people due to alcohol or drug addictions or criminal activity.)

We don't want you to shun your friends; instead, we want you to reach a point where you can reach out your hand to them, pull them up, and invite them to come on this journey with you. However, before you can do that, you need to make sure you have your own footing so you have the strength to do it.

Boundaries

Without a firm foundation to stand on, it will be all too easy to be pulled back down into the sins you are trying to overcome. As you continue to work on developing virtuous habits, you will need to be very cautious about situations that make it too difficult to live your convictions.

To prevent yourself from getting into a challenging situation, it is wise to place rules or boundaries on how you interact with your friends who don't always make virtuous choices. For example, if they are engaging in your triggers (partying, watching porn, having coed sleepovers), then don't hang out with them. That's a sure way to set yourself up for failure. Instead, find neutral activities you can enjoy together. Go out to coffee, work out together, catch a good movie you find mutually interesting, or invite them to come hang out with your friends who are striving for holiness.

We are not asking you to be your friends' savior. As you've already learned, even if you wanted to, you couldn't. What we are asking is that you be a friend who is willing to walk with them in their brokenness and love them enough to want to show them the way to peace and fulfillment.

Pray for your friends who need to know the love of Jesus in an authentic way. Ask God to give you the grace and strength you need to share his love with them and to open doors to make it possible.

Today's Detox Challenge

Today we suggest you create in your journal a list of rules and boundaries, as well as a backup exit plan, for when you are with your friends who can pull you down. One interviewee put it this way: "Good fighter pilots have rules for when they will eject if their plane is in trouble. They have to have the mentality locked in, and they follow through with it before it's too late."

What rules do you need to set so you don't find yourself in a troublesome situation? And if you do unintentionally find yourself there, how will you safely eject?

Be proactive in your thinking. For example, if you plan on visiting friends who sometimes engage in your trigger of drinking, call before you go to ask what they are up to. If you find out they are drinking, then don't go over there at that time. If they are not drinking, then text your accountability partner before you go so he or she can check in with you later, then drive yourself there so you can be in control of leaving if things change.

Day 30: What's the Point?

Throughout most of high school I (Lisa) was that girl who always had a boyfriend. As soon as one relationship would end, I was on the hunt for the next one to begin. To ensure that my search would never take too long, I had a backup plan: I could return to my on-again, off-again relationship with a guy named Alex.

When senior year came, we began to think about life after high school. Since we were both college bound, we began to explore our options. When I thought about college, I imagined myself settling into my picture-perfect dorm room, which looked like a page right out of a Pottery Barn catalogue. I imagined exploring my college town with my new BFFs, as we took spontaneous and impractical adventures that we would one day call epic. And I pictured myself in the midst of late-night cramming sessions with my classmates, downing black coffee and discussing how next time we'd plan ahead. In all this daydreaming I came to realize one thing: Alex was never in the picture.

This puzzled me at first. Alex almost always had a place in my high school experiences, and now as I looked forward to college, I didn't see him as a part of that equation. I paused as I realized that I didn't really care if we went to the same college. In truth, I didn't see him as a necessary part of my future.

A Game Changer

This knowledge brought me to a difficult reality: *eventually we would break up*. At first I thought the experiences and good memories that we had yet to make throughout our senior year would make it worth staying together. After all, wouldn't it make more sense to wait and break up with him at a natural time, like at some point in the summer before we left for college? What was so wrong with enjoying this relationship and growing from whatever experiences that came with it?

With this in mind, I tried to convince myself that there was still something I could gain from staying with Alex, but a nagging voice in my mind kept calling out, "*Eventually you will break up.*" No matter how hard I tried, my heart just wasn't in it anymore. I couldn't see the point in continuing to give my emotions, memories, and affections to a doomed relationship. I started to distance myself from Alex until finally I couldn't ignore the echo any longer. So, on the night of homecoming, we sat in his car when he drove me back home, and in an explosion of emotion, I broke up with Alex.

Reality Check

This is the reality of dating relationships: either they end in a breakup, or they last forever. As soon as I realized this, I began to look at my relationship with Alex differently. I asked myself if he could be my forever, my future spouse, and the father of my children. Once I realized that the answer was no, I couldn't bring my heart to stay with him when I knew we would eventually break up.

The world often tells us that the point of dating is to have fun, gain new experiences, and make memories. For a long time I bought into that mentality, until the reality that my heart was just not made for that was staring me in the face. I couldn't let the purpose of my dating be so shortsighted. If I was going to give of myself in such cherished ways, I at least needed to have hope that a future together might be a real possibility. If I was simply looking for fun and memories, couldn't that be gained in less intensive ways through friendships? It's not as though new experiences and personal growth can only be achieved through dating, right? Right.

With my new understanding of dating having an actual purpose, I wasn't willing to allow the avenue that would lead me to my future spouse to be based simply on fun and games, with the hope that in the end things would magically pan out. If I was going to date someone, then it was going to be with a purpose: a purpose of seeing if one day this person could truly be my forever, my one, my future husband.

Today's Detox Challenge

Today in your journal we suggest you make a list of people you either have or want to have a "more than friends" relationship with. The list should include any of the following people:

- An official boyfriend or girlfriend

- A person you are in an unofficial relationship with, but there is some level of romantic involvement between you

- An ex-boyfriend or ex-girlfriend you at least occasionally desire to get back together with

- A person you would like one day to be in a relationship with, but nothing has happened yet

- A person you are keeping around as a "backup"

We are going to come back to this list in a few days, so keep it close by.

Day 31: Starting Over

In small towns miles apart from each other, Ben and Rosie grew up with the same hardworking, Midwestern values. Although they were both raised Catholic, neither of them truly embraced their faith in a way that affected how they lived their lives. They each lost their virginity before graduating from high school and headed to college feeling slightly jaded by a world that failed to deliver the true love they were longing for.

A year after meeting through some mutual friends, Ben and Rosie started dating. Ben said, "We had both been in really broken relationships that were all about using each other. So when we started dating we desired to have a relationship that would look different from our past ones, but within two months we were sleeping together. We didn't feel too good about it, but we were doing what all our friends did and going through the motions of what typical college students do."

In their hearts they knew there had to be something more than what the world was giving them, but it wasn't until after hitting the one-year mark in their relationship that Ben felt that he had found the answer.

Acting a Bit Strange

Ben and Rosie occasionally attended Sunday Mass together, and it was there that Ben was introduced to a missionary named Marcus. Marcus began to invite Ben to hang out with him, and through their friendship, Ben began to want to change how he was living, especially in his relationship with Rosie.

At first Rosie thought Ben was acting a bit strange, but she was so intrigued by the changes that were going on in his life that she decided to start meeting with a female friend who, like Marcus, was striving to live her life for Christ. Seeing the authentic lives of their two friends left Ben and Rosie wanting more. Before long, they couldn't deny the way that Christ was pursuing their hearts.

Rosie told us, "We decided that we needed to go to daily Mass. We didn't know why, but we knew it was something we should be doing. At the same time, we were still sleeping together, which really started wrestling with our hearts."

Wrestling

To answer that wrestling, Ben and Rosie finally decided to try to stop sleeping together. Ben said, "It was really hard because we were like, 'Whoa, sex is how we show love and affection. How's that going to look?' It's all we knew—it's how all our friends were doing it."

Despite their hesitation, they began to back away from their physical relationship. Ben recounted, "At first we said, 'Okay, we won't have sex, but we can still have each other stay over for the night.' When that didn't work, we thought, 'Okay we'll just make out,' but that didn't work either. We figured out that it didn't work because when we'd have the physical touch, we'd find ourselves wanting to do more."

This struggle went on until they finally decided that if they wanted to be serious about setting things straight, then they needed to place some pretty hefty parameters on their relationship in order to build the virtues needed to live a chaste relationship. Ben explained, "If we needed to not hold hands, that was worth it. If at the end of the night I just needed to drop Rosie off and leave right away, we would do that." Whatever it took, they were ready and willing to make the sacrifices necessary to be truly free to love each other.

Changes

Ben and Rosie continued to attend daily Mass and they began to pray together as a couple, asking God for the grace to live a chaste relationship. When they did fall into their old sins, they immediately turned to Confession and courageously began again. They sought out holy dating and married couples who could model for them what authentic relationships should look like and, even when it was scary, they earnestly asked God to reveal his will to them.

"At one point we realized that we'd never pursued the Lord as singles. We'd never learned to allow him to fill our hearts as singles," Rosie shared. "So we asked, 'Is this really what the Lord desires, or should we break up?'"

"I had never considered the priesthood," Ben chimed in, "and Rosie had never asked the Lord if she was called to the religious life."

While asking these tough questions, Ben and Rosie humbled themselves by seeking out their faith-filled mentors and friends for guidance, and confronted these issues head-on, trusting that the Lord would lead them.

As challenging as it all may sound, it worked. For the next two and a half years Ben and Rosie grew in holiness. After giving up all physical affection for a time, they were able to reintroduce acts of affection that conveyed love and not use. Through God's grace they were able love each other with Christ-like love, and they succeeded in not engaging in sexual intimacy ... until their wedding night.

Take Hope

We love Ben and Rosie's story because it is a story of hope. It is a story that proves that God can take a relationship that is broken and twisted and make it new. The road was not always easy for them, and at times they felt very alone in their journey, but they will tell you that it was worth it. If you find yourself in a similar situation, take hope. God can do wonderful things with hearts that are willing to follow his plan.

Now What?

When asking Ben and Rosie what advice they would give to a couple in their situation, they relayed many of the things you have already read about. Know your weaknesses and have someone hold you accountable for them. Your relationship with the Lord must come first and foremost because only he can satisfy the deepest longings of your heart. Be honest with Jesus in prayer and don't listen to the lies of the devil, who will try to tell you that you've already gone too far. Be rooted in prayer and the Sacraments. Continue to come back to the Lord's love and mercy as you work to overcome sin.

All of these things are necessary to live chastely, but one piece of advice stood out from all the rest: both people in the relationship have to want it.

"If you are not both seeking the Lord, how will you be able to have a pure relationship?" Rosie asked. "If they're not willing to listen to you when you say we need to stop doing this, if you get married one day, how will they be able to lead you to Heaven?"

If you are serious about wanting to live in the freedom that comes with chastity, know that a couple can start over, but the key is that they have to be willing to do it together.

Today's Detox Challenge

In today's chapter Rosie asked how anyone will be able to lead another to Heaven one day if the person can't even make sacrifices while dating.

Whether you are single or in a serious relationship, you can start working on being a sacrificial man or woman who can lead another to Heaven by voluntarily denying yourself in small ways.

Today we challenge you to deny your flesh a small comfort for twenty-four hours for the sake of practicing sacrifice. Here are some ideas for things you might pick:

- Give up media for the day.

- Don't lean on the back of a chair or on a table (sit like you are on a bench).

- Don't scratch itches.

- Sleep without a pillow.

- Put a pebble in your shoe.

- Refrain from using warm water (for showers, hand washing, and so on).

- Give up looking at your phone while you're walking from place to place.

Day 32: Letting Go

Teresa got involved in her youth group in high school because of the cute guys and cool trips. She heard the message of chastity, but it didn't click until she heard it from a new perspective at a Catholic young adult conference, which unfortunately was after she had already begun sleeping with her boyfriend, John.

"I was angry in one of the talks because the speaker was telling beautiful stories of people who saved themselves for marriage. It hurt because I didn't have that, and I felt like I had been used," explained Teresa.

At the end of the talk the speaker told the audience that if a person really loves them, then rather than use their body, they would reverence it. This gave Teresa a glimmer of hope. Perhaps once she explained chastity to John, they could start again?

"I went home and told him, 'I think we should practice purity,'" Teresa told us. "He agreed to it, but it only lasted a few days, and then he began to pout. He'd tell me things like 'I don't know how to love you any other way than by having sex with you,' and I believed him."

Teresa was torn. She wanted chastity *and* John, but it didn't appear that she could have both. In her unwillingness to lose John, she caved, and things went back to normal.

Transforming

In the midst of this internal battle, Teresa found herself developing her prayer life, going to Mass, and getting involved in the Catholic community on her campus. It was there that she began to make friends with people who seemed genuinely interested in her as a person. She also saw firsthand what authentic dating relationships looked like, and she noticed that the men there respected her and weren't just looking to get with her.

As Teresa's life began to transform, the divide between her and John widened. Soon they started going through an agonizing cycle of breaking up and getting back together, as Teresa's desire to live a chaste life simply would not go away.

"What Do You Have in Common?"

On a crisp fall afternoon, Teresa was invited to grab coffee with a new friend. After nestling into a cozy spot in the café, they began chatting and the topic of John came up. Her friend casually asked, "So tell me, what do you and John have in common?" Teresa paused for a moment, "Well, um … ," she sputtered, struggling to find an answer.

"Then it hit me," Teresa said. "For the first time I thought, 'Wow, I don't know if we are really meant to be together forever.'"

Felt Like Love

Facing this reality was incredibly scary for Teresa. She had already made a significant physical and emotional investment in John by giving him her heart and her body. Now that certain memories had been made, physical acts had been shared, and emotional depths had been reached, it was hard to imagine walking away from it all. Even though things weren't as good as she had hoped they'd be, admitting that she might have been wrong about John was unbearable.

Teresa explained, "I had trusted John with so much, and what we had *felt* like love. I knew in my mind and in my heart that God wanted better, but the bond I had with him was very strong. I was afraid that I had found 'the one' and that if I let him go I would spend the rest of my life alone with regret."

Again she was torn. She still wanted chastity and John, but this time she was ready to choose chastity over John.

"I knew we needed to break up. I started going to Eucharistic Adoration to try to get the strength. In prayer I said, 'Jesus if you want this you have to help me do it because I have tried before, and I have failed.'"

It was then that God whispered to her, "Be not afraid, and trust in my promise of Jeremiah 29:11." This was a verse that Teresa knew, but struggled to take to heart. "For I know the plans I have for you, says the Lord, plans for welfare and not for evil, to give you a future and a hope" (Jeremiah 29:11).

For the first time the words sank in, and Teresa finally gained the confidence she needed to trust that God would take care of her. After that encounter, she broke up with John for a final time.

God Has a Plan

Have you ever been there? Like Teresa, have you ever been afraid to let go of a relationship? Maybe it wasn't even a relationship that was necessarily bad for you but one you just knew wasn't right. If so, we understand. It's scary to walk away from something without knowing what will come after, but it's in moments like these that you have to trust that God's words in Jeremiah 29:11 are not just a line. They are a promise—a promise that God has a plan for you because he loves you.

If you are praying, seeking sound counsel, frequenting the Sacraments, and doing what you are called to do right now, God will not abandon you as he leads you along the path to discovering your call in life, whether it is to marriage, the single life, or to the priesthood or religious life.

It is true that because you have free will, sometimes you may deviate from God's best plan for you—but don't let that paralyze you. God is your loving Father and he can use even your mistakes for good. Do not be afraid. If you take a wrong turn, God will not leave you on the wrong path. Rather, like a GPS system, he will simply redirect you to a new path that will get you to where he desires you to go.

Today's Detox Challenge

It took Teresa nine months to admit that John was not right for her, and in two ways. First, he was not what she wanted. Second, he was not what she needed. They had nothing in common and, in the end, he didn't make her a better person.

Today we invite you to turn to the page in your journal titled "Is it really so?" from Day 23. On this page you have already listed some non-negotiable characteristics that you *want* from a person. Now we want you to add to the list any other characteristics that you *need* from a person.

Your list may include things such as: someone who will push me to strive for excellence, someone who will be sensitive to the ways my parents' divorce still affects me, or someone who will help balance my workaholic tendencies.

Knowing what you need from a person is not a bad or selfish thing. This kind of knowledge can prevent disappointment and is very helpful in determining if you could truly be compatible with someone in the lifelong commitment of marriage.

Finally, keep in mind with both today's list and your list from Day 23 that if you are not reasonable and/or realistic with your wants and needs, then your expectations may be too high. We are not asking you to lower your standards; rather we are asking you to avoid making your list *too* specific ("must love ferrets, indie rock, and be willing to attend a minimum of twenty Royals games per season") or too shallow ("must have blue eyes, chestnut hair, and an incredible singing voice"). These are likely not legitimate wants and needs, but rather personal preferences that in the end are just that—preferences.

Day 33: Ben and Rosie, or Teresa and John?

We began this week by looking at the purpose of dating, which is to enter into a relationship with the intent of discovering if you could one day marry this person. We followed this up by looking at the reality that every relationship ends in one of two ways: either a couple breaks up like Teresa and John or they stay together forever like Ben and Rosie.

Now we invite you to pull out the list of names that you created on Day 30. On this list you wrote down people who fit into any of the following categories:

- An official boyfriend or girlfriend

- A person you are in an unofficial relationship with, but there is some level of romantic involvement between you

- An ex-boyfriend or ex-girlfriend you at least occasionally desire to get back together with

- A person you would like one day to be in a relationship with, but nothing has happened yet

- A person you are keeping around as a "backup"

As you look at this list we want you to ask yourself, "Is there a reasonable hope for a real future with some or any of the individuals on this list?" To help you answer this question, we have come up with a list of "green lights" and "red lights" that you can consider in evaluating this question for each person.

Green Lights

Beginning with the first name on your list, read the first green-light statement and ask yourself, "Is this true for this person?"

If you can truly answer "yes", then put one tally mark next to the person's name. If you are unsure, *do not* draw a mark. Then, read the next green-light statement and evaluate it in the same manner. Continue in this way until you have evaluated each statement for the first person on your list. When you are finished, go through the same process with the next person on your list, and so on, until you have considered each person.

- Your relationship is based on willing the good of each other.

- This person desires to pursue a chaste life.

- When you think about the future, you can see him or her as a part of it.

- He or she meets your list of non-negotiable wants and needs. (Days 23 and 32)

- The love you share strives to imitate free, faithful, total, and life-giving Trinitarian love, as appropriate to your relationship right now.

- You mutually support each other emotionally.

- He or she seeks spiritual growth apart from you.

- This person has engaged in a community that challenges each individual to grow in holiness.

- Your family and friends do not express concern about your relationship.

Answering "yes" to most of the green lights for an individual person is an indicator that there could be a reasonable hope for a real future with that person, and that he or she is likely the kind of person who could help you grow in virtue and holiness.

If any names on your list do not have at least five tally marks next to them, cross them off the list. Even if it's hard and you don't want to, we suggest you just do it.

Please keep in mind: this list has nothing to do with whether or not this person is actually a good or practical match for you. Just because someone has enough tallies from the green-light list does not mean that you two should marry. It simply means that at this time, it is safe for you to consider beginning or continuing a relationship with this person.

Red Lights

Now, beginning again with the first name on your list, read the first red-light statement and ask yourself, "Is this true for this person?" If you can truly answer "yes" to the statement, then put a tally mark next to the person's name. If you are unsure about a statement, *also* put a tally mark. Then, read the next red-light statement and evaluate it in the same manner. Continue in this way until you have evaluated each statement for the first person on your list. When you are finished, go through the same process with the next person on your list, and so on, until you have considered each person.

- Your relationship is based on physical or emotional use.

- He or she claims to support your stance on chastity but pressures you to be unchaste.

- When you think about the future, you are unsure whether you want him or her to be a part of it.

- This person fails to meet at least some items on your list of non-negotiable wants and needs (Days 23 and 31).

- He or she supports your faith but has no interest in pursuing a faith of his or her own.

* The emotional needs of this person consistently leave you feeling burned out and drained.

* He or she only attends faith-related events to please you.

* This person pulls you away from your faith, family, or friends.

* Fear is a factor that keeps your relationship together.

Answering "yes" to most of the red lights is an indicator that at this time there is not a reasonable hope for a real future with this person. It is also probable that beginning or continuing a relationship with this person will prevent you from growing in holiness and finding the peace and joy you are searching for.

If any names on your list have at least five tally marks next to them (not including the tally marks from the green light list), cross them off the list. Again, even if it's hard and you don't want to, we suggest you just do it.

Please keep in mind: it is possible for people to change, and given time, there may be a reasonable hope for a real future with someone you just crossed off. However, do not let this be the reason that you do not cross a person off your list because at this time the reasonable hope is not there. Staying with or starting something new with someone because "maybe this person might one day change" is a recipe for failure. Let who the person is right now be your determining factor. You don't want to date someone for who you *want* him or her to be in the future, because that might never happen. If someone is going to change, the person needs to do it because it is what he or she wants, not because it is what you want.

Today's Detox Challenge

This is the challenge that you probably hoped we'd never give. Take a deep breath and say a quick prayer. You know where we are going with this.

Who did you cross off your list?

Is it time? Is it time to let go?

If there isn't a reasonable hope for a real future, then why continue to give parts of yourself to this person? Physically, emotionally, mentally—why invest in or hold on to something that will never come together or will eventually fall apart?

For some of you, this letting go will mean getting someone out of your heart; for others it will require completely removing someone from your life. This. Is. Hard. We know, and our hearts are heavy for you, but we want you to be free: free to become the holy man or woman God is calling you to be and free to love and be loved.

Right now we invite you to take the first step in letting go. If your act of letting go is only in your mind and heart, consider deleting these people from your phone, removing them from your social media feeds, and stopping mentally stalking them. Pray about whatever you need to do to help you move on.

If this letting go requires physically letting go or a breakup, consider sending the person a text right now to ask if you can set up a time to talk. If you know you can't do it in person, then maybe writing a letter is a better option. Whatever makes sense for your circumstances, ask God for the strength to start the process right now.

You can do it. You need to do it. Be not afraid—God has a plan for your life. He loves you. Trust him.

Day 34: From Friends to Dating

Let's be honest—yesterday's chapter was probably intense for you. If you are still mustering up the courage to do what you know you need to do, remember, you are a person with an immortal soul who was created in the image of an all-powerful God who wants to fill you with the peace of living in his perfect will. As you continue to work through this part of the process, keep praying, call on your accountability partner or a friend for support (especially if you are doubting your decision), and make sure you are taking care of yourself.

My Pseudo

During my senior year in high school, I (Kevin) started to become friends with Rebecca. At first, we just began to talk more during youth group; then we quickly found ways to hang out all the time.

It was pretty obvious that there was an attraction between us, but I was a senior, and she was a sophomore. I knew that I'd be heading off to college soon, and I wasn't quite sure how I felt about a long-distance relationship. I had a choice to make: either to date Rebecca despite the distance or to scale back our relationship to the level of friendship. Which would I choose?

I chose ... well, not to make a choice. Instead, Rebecca and I began a confusing three-year cycle of relationship ambiguity. I would often say that we were just friends, but my friends, who saw right through me, called her my "pseudo," which was short for pseudo girlfriend. At the end of the three years, I "broke up" with Rebecca, even though we weren't officially dating. Think about that for a moment. ...

Rebecca and I wasted a lot of time, energy, and emotion on our relationship. Sometimes in relationships this happens even with the best intentions, but I let it happen because I wasn't willing to make a decision. Instead, I selfishly held Rebecca in suspense and then crushed her with my decision. I knew I wanted to handle my next relationship differently.

Defining the Relationship

Picture this: it's my junior year in college, and I'm driving back to campus with Lisa from our hometown. We aren't dating yet ,and I'm a bit nervous about what's about to take place. I'm not quite sure how to say it, and I don't quite know how she will react. I do know that what I'm about to say will help define who we are and what our future together will be.

You see, Lisa and I had known each other for a few years, but over the last couple of months we had spent a lot of time together by carpooling, hanging out with a group of mutual friends, and occasionally running together as she trained for a marathon. I realized that it was time to talk about our relationship, and when we were within ten minutes of campus, I let her know ... that I was glad that we were just friends.

At the time, I didn't quite know how I felt about Lisa, and I didn't want to do the same thing I did with Rebecca. Later Lisa told me that she was disappointed, but it actually made things a lot easier because at least she knew where we stood.

Something Changed

But, as time went on, something changed. I came to know her character—the way she approached life, her devotion to her family, her love for children, and most important, her love for Our Lord. Oh, and I realized more and more just how physically beautiful she was. That didn't hurt either!

As my heart began to change, I realized that I needed to readdress our relationship, but the stakes were high. Asking out a person you know you will see again can be hard. And I knew I would see Lisa a lot in the future—by this time, I had signed up to run the marathon with her! Imagine running together for four hours with someone who turned you down!

Despite the potential costs, as we were stretching to run, I let her know how I felt. Given the way I had previously handled the situation, Lisa was incredibly surprised but happily agreed to let me take her on a date.

Application

We hope you've learned a thing or two from my successes and failures in approaching dating relationships. Through these two stories, I want to point out some key takeaways to think about as your relationships move from friends to dating.

Awareness: The first thing to keep in mind is that you have to be aware of what's happening in your relationships. How much time, energy, and thought are you giving to a person of the opposite sex? What signals are you sending?

This doesn't mean you can't hang out with members of the opposite sex—that's how people begin to date! But you do need to be aware of the situation as it progresses.

Know where you want to take the relationship:
As you become aware of what's going on in a particular situation, you might need to ask yourself, "What is my hope for this relationship?" Then follow up that question with: "Do my words and actions reflect this desire?"

When we've just met someone, many times we aren't sure what we want for the relationship. This is totally normal. However, our words and actions should reflect this. With Rebecca, I didn't know where I wanted to take the relationship. But my words and actions said, "I really would like to date you."

Decision time: As you move from friends to dating, there is always a moment when you actually need to define the relationship. It's a balancing act not to do this too soon or too late. With Rebecca, I was painfully late. With Lisa, I think I was right on time both in my declaration of friendship and in my later invitation to date.

Advice to Men

In Ephesians, St. Paul describes the dynamics of a married relationship. He says, "Husbands, love your wives, as Christ loved the Church and gave himself up for her" (Ephesians 5:25). How did Christ love the Church? He died for her! If the goal of dating is marriage, then our dating relationships need to start with us men sacrificing for the women we love.

When it comes to defining relationships, men take a cue from our culture and many times fail to commit. Why? It is because we would rather not risk rejection. We'd rather just go with the flow and see what happens. This is what I did with Rebecca. This is what boys do. Men step up to the plate and are willing to sacrifice their reputation and hearts instead of making women suffer in ambiguity.

Advice to Women

If we added up the time between when a guy should ask a girl out and when he actually does, we could probably take all that time and energy and solve world hunger. I know this is difficult, but it is so important that you begin your relationship by allowing the guy to sacrifice for you. If he doesn't at the start of the relationship, it probably won't get any better.

This doesn't mean you don't have any influence or control in the situation. If you see a continual pattern in which a guy demonstrates that he likes you but fails to ask you out, feel free to ask him to define the relationship before moving forward, or to stop hanging out with him as much.

Also, we've heard many examples in which the guy will not commit, and as a result, the girl resorts to using physical affection in the hope that it will convince the guy to make a commitment. This only reinforces the cycle. If a guy can be physical with you without dating you, then he doesn't see any reason to commit. Don't fall into this trap!

Today's Detox Challenge

Are you currently in a relationship that needs to be defined? Today we challenge you to send that person a text right now asking when you can get together to talk.

Day 35: God Has a Plan

For my sixteenth birthday I (Lisa) asked for a chastity ring. When I worried or struggled with that decision, I wrote love letters to my future husband, prayed for him, and blasted Carolyn Dawn Johnson's "One Day Closer to You"[1] in the car.

> So, I'm not gonna worry
> No, I'm in no hurry
> It's in the hands of fate, there's nothing I can do
> And it might be tomorrow
> Or the one that follows
> Got the rest of my life to look forward to
> 'Cause every day is one day closer to you
>
> Oh, every day I pray that God will keep you safe
> 'Cause I know you're out there somewhere

Each of these things helped me to move past my struggles and gave meaning to why I was doing what I was doing. However, these pull-yourself-together-and-focus activities made a large assumption, and it would have devastated me if it never became a reality. The assumption was simply this: that God's plan for me *was* marriage.

Like so many of my friends, I expected that eventually I would get married. It was never a question of *if*, only a question of *when*. For me the *when* came quickly, but for many of my friends the *when* took years longer, and for others the *when* still hasn't arrived. The truth is, it might not ever.

Nowhere in the Bible does it say, "and God created for each man a woman to one day be his spouse." That's an assumption that many of us have made and it can be a very dangerous one. For some people, God's plan will be a call to the priesthood or religious life, and for others, it will be a call to remain single always. Yes, you might not ever get married.

Whomp, Whomp, Whomp

Here we are, almost at the end of a book on how to reorder your understanding of love and dating *so you can be free to love and be loved*, and I just dropped that bomb on you. Cruel? I hope notbecause this truth is not meant to depress you or send you into a downward spiral of fear and anxiety. Actually, I hope it will save you from fear and anxiety. Not convinced? Read on.

The C Word

Two days before I left for college, my family was struck with the news that my dad had cancer. At the time, the doctors had high hopes of putting him into remission, but it was in a daze that my parents drove me an hour north of my home to Benedictine College. Days rolled by, and his doctors began implementing their plan to heal him, but after every treatment the news was always the same: it's not working. Soon it became clear that my dad's cancer could not be cured, and he was labeled terminal.

My dad, Brian, was not always a saint, but in my opinion his illness made him into one. He filled his days praying the Rosary, studying the Catholic Faith, volunteering any energy he had to help out Catholic organizations, and hollering at priests passing by his hospital room to get in there and hear his confession. Our family and community at large all prayed with him as well, begging God for a miracle.

If He Just Had More

During my sophomore year, my friends and I were talking about my dad's battle, and one of them said, "You know Lisa, if your dad just had more faith, then God would heal him."

Immediately my body tensed up. "Do you mean to tell me that the reason my dad hasn't been healed is because he doesn't believe in God enough?" I shot back.

"Yep," he responded confidently. "He just needs to believe and pray, and God will heal him."

The words "*if your dad just had more faith*" seethed in my mind as my blood started to boil. This guy didn't even know my dad. My dad had faith. He breathed faith. He wanted desperately to be healed. And yet this guy was telling me that it was his *lack of faith* that kept him terminally ill.

Junior year came and with it my dad's last moment on earth. Ten priests, an abbot, and an archbishop all concelebrated his funeral Mass. Nearly two dozen men, many of whom claimed that my dad was *their* best friend, served as pallbearers. Those who had been praying for him packed the large church till it was standing room only.

The man who just needed more faith to be healed died.

God's Desires, Our Desires

Let's be clear: I'm not saying that never getting married is like getting cancer. What I am saying is that God's desires are not always our desires. Praying harder or mustering up more faith does not equate to God giving us what *we think* we want or need.

God is not a genie.

Sadly, various forms of this false "health and wealth gospel" — the message that if you have enough faith you will get what you want—are often fed to singles as they patiently wait for God to bring them a spouse: "Just keep waiting and praying. Of course God will bring you a spouse!" Yet God never made that promise, so time passes by and they begin to wonder, "What am I doing wrong? Does God even care?"

We don't want you to live your life thinking that you've somehow messed things up and that it's your fault that you're not married yet. We don't want you assuming that there must be something wrong with you, that "God is *still* working to prepare you for your future spouse" (as if you're some special project that's indefinitely too messed up to handle a real relationship, so just keep trying to get holier, okay?). Finally, we don't want you anxiously wasting your life waiting for something that may or may not be God's plan anyway.

There will be times in your life when you desire something good, but for one reason or another, God does not fulfill that desire in the way you expect him to. At times it will be made clear to you why he has chosen to act as he has, and at other times the life he is presenting to you will seem like a mystery. The key is not to despair but to trust that God is always working and that he has a plan and a *will* for your life.

Thy Will Be Done

God wants you to ask for the good things you desire. He wants you to be real with him in your prayers. He wants you to tell him about your fears and your struggles because when you are real with God, he can be real with you. It is in that vulnerability that you can open yourself up in a way that allows God to show you his will.

So, yes, continue to ask and pray that God will ... but at the same time, pray *for* God's will. We're not asking you to give up; we're asking you to ask for the grace to abandon your desires to the desires of your Father. Ask him to conform your heart to his because it is in wanting what God wants that you find peace. It is through living in God's will that you find joy. It might not be what you are expecting, but if you can do his will, it will be even better than your original plans.

Today's Detox Challenge

Today we propose you write a letter ... to Jesus. Ask him with great confidence for the things that you desire, but make sure to ask him that if they are not his desires that he change your heart to match his. And at the end of the day, "Thy will be done."

Discussion Questions for Week 5

1. One of the challenges this week was to find ways to make sacrifices. What sacrifices have you made in the past? What's been really hard? What's been effective?

2. On Day 33, we list "green lights" and "red lights" that you can consider in evaluating people you might date. Did any of these stand out to you?

3. Before reading this book, would you have looked at these lists the same way you do now? What has changed?

4. Have you ever walked away from a serious relationship? What was hard about letting go? What helped you make your decision? Were you tempted to get back together?

5. On Day 34, Kevin identified several tips for taking relationships from friendship to dating. Did any of the tips surprise you? Do you think you will approach your next relationship differently as it moves from friendship to dating?

6. What's the most difficult part about waiting for a spouse? How does this waiting process affect your relationship with God?

WEEK 6: MOVING FORWARD

Last week we took a look at the point of dating, and we challenged you to let go of the relationships in your life that do not have a reasonable hope for a future together. (Please don't continue to hate us for that. It's for the best; we promise.) You read about the process of going from friendship to dating, and we challenged you to consider the fact that not everyone will get married.

This is it—the final five days of your journey. During this time, we will be looking at some important factors that will play into your confidence regarding being free to love and be loved. You have worked hard to get to where you are, and we want to ensure that you have the ability not just to maintain your progress, but also to build upon it.

Day 36: Healing

The most difficult part about writing this book was hearing the stories that we are going to share with you today. They are the stories of interviewees who were in need of healing, not because of the things they had done but because of the things that had been done to them.

We heard from Natalie, who had her virginity taken from her by her boyfriend, but because of her emotional attachment to him, she stuck with him for the next three years. We heard from Amy, who while making an overnight campus visit to her top choice for college was given a date-rape drug at a party and woke up the next morning in a stranger's dorm room. We heard from Emily Ann, who was sexually abused as a child by someone she should have been able to trust. We heard from Michael, whose girlfriend seduced and manipulated him into being intimate with her. We heard from Elizabeth, who was gang-raped while she was blacked out at a party with people she thought were her friends.

The list of those we interviewed who had been taken advantage of was alarmingly long, and their stories were painfully difficult to hear. However, at the end of each story there was hope: hope and a path toward healing in the hearts of each individual whose dignity and worth was not upheld. Through the grace of God, they each were able to face their scars and find ways to move forward without being paralyzed or defined by their past.

The pain that comes from being taken advantage of or abused is real. We wish we could give you a foolproof formula for fixing things, but that is simply not possible. The path to healing is personal, and only you can take it. There is absolutely no way we can bring you to a point of healing in this one short chapter, but we can help you take some first steps.

Face It

When memories of painful experiences rise up, it's understandable why you might want to run from them and try to pretend they never happened. Nevertheless, this sweep-it-under-the-rug-and-act-like-it's-not-there approach does nothing to address the problem; it actually makes it worse. If you want to heal from the past, you have to face it. As hard as it is, you have to allow what happened to be brought into the light and then deal with it head-on. The good news is that you don't have to deal with it alone.

You Need Jesus

Standing at the door of your heart is a Divine Physician who is patiently knocking and waiting for you to let him in and tell him where it hurts. He wants to do the work of healing you; however, he is a perfect gentleman, and he will only come in if he is invited. If you want to be healed by him, you have to ask.

You have to invite Jesus into those darker moments and ask him to reveal where he was and how to help you move forward.

"I try to invite Jesus to heal me every day," Natalie told us. "I say, 'Lord, what do you want to heal in me today?' It's a process because if Jesus completely healed me all at once I wouldn't be able to handle it. He desires to heal us, and he knows what needs to be healed. He also knows the right order to do it in."

Sometimes your healing will be focused on striving to forgive those who hurt you. Sometimes it will be focused on learning how to accept your past but not let it consume you. Sometimes it will be focused on trying to love yourself and know your true worth and dignity. Only Jesus can know what you need in each moment, so you have to let him do his work, even when you don't feel like it … especially when you don't feel like it.

Although this approach to ongoing healing isn't always easy, it's important. As you consistently make efforts to heal, Jesus will be able to reveal to you how your scars are affecting you right now, and he will be able to show you ways to take the next step on your journey.

Be Patient with Yourself

As we said, healing is a process that is never really complete; rather, it's a series of continual transformations, so you need to learn to be patient with yourself and the process.

Many of the interviewees we spoke with acknowledged this reality. "Sometimes I get frustrated and think, 'Why am I not over it?'" Natalie confessed as she shared her struggle to forgive the people who hurt her. "It took me five years to want to be touched again," explained Amy as she talked about allowing male friends to get near her. "I find it hard for a guy to pursue me because I was taken control of, and I want to be the one who is in control now," Emily Ann shared about striving to move beyond being abused as a child. When dealing with difficult scars like these, being patient with yourself is not easy, but with the help of Jesus, incremental healing is possible.

Hope. Always hope. God is always working and he wants to bring you to a place of peace with your past. Continually invite him in, and he will do the rest.

Don't Try to Heal Alone

Although Jesus is always the ultimate healer, oftentimes it is helpful to bring other people into the process. This is where a spiritual director or faith-based professional counselor can be extremely helpful. (Visit us at madetomagnify.com for a list of where to find a sound Catholic counselor.)

When someone can walk with you on the path to healing, he or she can point out things you may not be able to see on your own, teach you skills that will help you cope with continuing struggles, and offer support so you know that you are not alone.

"If you have ever thought, 'Maybe I should go to counseling,' then go," advised Natalie. "We all have baggage, and there is nothing shameful about going. It's never too late, and it doesn't have to be forever."

Today's Detox Challenge

Today we want you to consider Natalie's advice. If you have ever thought that possibly you should go to counseling, then we suggest you seriously look into going. To start, meet with a trusted priest, religious, lay spiritual director, or mentor and ask for help assessing whether meeting with a professional counselor would be beneficial for you. You can also consider meeting with a spiritual director and seeing a counselor at the same time. For many of the interviewees we spoke with, this was a helpful formula for walking along the path of healing. However you choose to move forward, make sure you are moving forward and do not let your scars plague you for the rest of your life.

Day 37: Emptiness

It took until his senior year of high school for Alfred to move from being friends with Arianna to dating her. Although he was graduating that May and she still had another year of high school, they decided to stay together and navigate the waters of a long-distance relationship. During that year, Alfred had a reversion to his Catholic Faith, which Arianna happily supported.

Their relationship began to transform, and after Arianna graduated, she joined Alfred at college. Even though she wasn't Catholic, she began to attend Mass with him, became a member of a Catholic Bible study, and eventually began going to RCIA classes.

Alfred wanted nothing more than for Arianna to join him in full participation in the Catholic Faith, so he thought he should be elated—yet something was not quite right, and he knew it. Fearing that if they broke up, Arianna would never get to experience the joy of the Sacraments and all that the Church has to offer, Alfred tried to ignore the disquiet that was creeping into his heart. Besides, why would he give up what they had? They were leading a chaste relationship and both growing in holiness—what more could he want?

Despite his best efforts, the uneasiness wouldn't go away, and Alfred finally did what he knew he had to do. After being together for three and a half years, Alfred placed his trust in God and broke up with Arianna.

Proud of himself for having the courage to be obedient to the promptings of God, Alfred took a deep breath and waited for God's peace to flood over him. Much to his surprise, the peace didn't come. So Alfred waited. Then he waited some more. Then he began to wonder.

The Aftermath

Over the last two weeks we have told you that Jesus is the only one who can fill the emptiness and heal the brokenness in your life. These aren't just cute Christian lines—they are some of the deepest truths that can be found this side of Heaven. We will forever stand by them, but we also want you to know that just because these things are true doesn't mean that you will always *feel* as if they are true.

There will be times in your life when Jesus will feel incredibly close and you will know that he is there. Yet there will also be times when he will feel incredibly far away, and you will doubt if he was ever there to begin with. This is the painful place Alfred found himself in the aftermath of his breakup with Arianna.

Alfred explained, "There were times when I wanted to get back together with her or find someone to fill the void. I would try to pray and spend more time with God, but I still just felt empty. Sometimes I would go out for a smoke break in the middle of the night and just stare at the stars and ask God, 'Why?' I would wonder about my life and what he had planned. I felt so smalland like God was just letting me squirm."

Emptiness

The emptiness that you will experience from time to time, even as a Christian who has given your life to Christ, is real. You will have moments when God will ask you to sit in the emptiness, waiting and wondering for an uncomfortably long period of time. In these moments it will be tempting to think you've been duped and want to give up, but that's exactly when you need to hold on.

Feeling Distant

As you read on Day 22, if good or positive feelings are taken away in a dating relationship, then it can be easy to think that your shared love has gone with them. However, feelings alone do not equal love. They are a part of love, but they are not love itself. This same principle applies to our relationship with God.

There will be times when God will *feel* distant, but just because you don't feel his presence doesn't mean he is not there. At times like this, your love for God is given a chance to become real because your love for him is not based on feelings; it's based on an act of the will. Love is a choice, even when it comes to God. It is in your darkest times that you are given a chance to *choose* to love and trust God, even when you don't feel like it.

As Alfred came to the realization that his love for God could not be based on feelings, instead of running from the emptiness, he learned to embrace it.

"I stopped being uncomfortable with the void I was feeling because I recognized that it was only something that I was feeling and perceiving, but I knew full well that God was there. I knew he was listening and that I could talk to him whenever I needed him."

Getting Real

With nowhere else to go, in his desperation Alfred began to get real with God in his prayer. He spoke to him from the depths of his heart in a way he never had before. He stopped worrying about pious pretenses and was brutally honest with God for the first time.

"I started to invite [God] into the depths of my life ... into my pain and loneliness. When I was finally honest with God and put my trust in him fulfilling me—that was when I could finally be honest with myself and start healing."

By allowing Alfred to feel deeply lonely and empty, God was offering him an opportunity to lean on and trust in him in an even deeper way. It was through his struggles that Alfred learned to rely on God and be authentic with him. In the end, God wasn't trying to push Alfred away. He was trying to draw him even closer.

Oftentimes it is in your lowest moments that God can do his best work. In your moments of despair, which *will* come, do not be afraid. God has not abandoned you; he's right there inviting you to come nearer so he can be your strength.

Today's Detox Challenge

In talking about the emotional suffering that can follow after a breakup, Teresa from Day 32 had this idea to share: "It is easy after a breakup to romanticize the relationship when you begin to feel lonely or unlovable, and it may seem like you made a mistake, but that is when it is important to remember the reasons why you broke up. I wrote in my journal all the reasons why my ex-boyfriend just wasn't good for me. Writing these things down helped me to snap out of it when I was lonely."

If you are still struggling to let go of a particular person you know is not right for you, try doing what Teresa did and write down a list of why this person is not right for you. Pull it out when you are feeling empty and read it over. Then try to be brutally honest with Jesus in your prayer and choose to trust in him, even if you don't feel like it.

Day 38: Fear

Rachel

In high school, Rachel was the only virgin among her group of friends, a fact that she was constantly teased for. "When's Rachel gonna get laid?" "Just do it and get it over with, then it won't be a big deal," they would taunt. Wanting to fit in, Rachel would often use vulgar language around her friends to try to appear "normal." She was also addicted to masturbating and creating her own sexual fantasies, which were actions that she didn't know were wrong.

After years of fighting off the pressure from her friends to "get it over with," Rachel finally gave in and slept with her boyfriend of two months. "I think I did it because I felt the pressure so badly, and I just wanted to be in the club," she recounted. "I basically used the guy and shortly after, we broke up."

Despite not being Catholic, Rachel decided to go on a retreat that her siblings had recommended to her. It was there that she learned for the first time that her actions were separating her from the love of God in ways that were making her miserable. She desired to make changes, but at that point her sexual lifestyle was so deep-seated that she didn't know where to begin. Over time and with the support and witness of amazing friends, Rachel eventually converted to Catholicism and began to gain control over her passions in ways that allowed her to start living the virtue of chastity.

Despite her successes, one thing still worried Rachel. Given her past mistakes, how could she possibly be lovable?

"There's this deep-rooted worry in me," Rachel said "Will a man ever love me? There are so many great guys who I do missionary work with and sometimes I look at them and think, 'There is no way some of them would ever want to be with me.'"

Andrew

When Andrew started dating Kim, he quickly realized that she had no convictions about the morality of physical intimacy. For Andrew, who was raised Catholic and had been taught that sexual acts were for marriage, this created an interesting moral dilemma.

"I would use her physically but tell myself the lie that as long as *she* was okay with it and I wasn't *forcing* her to do anything she didn't want to do, it was okay. But deep down, I knew this was wrong," Andrew explained.

Given time, Andrew was no longer able to cope with the way he was justifying his actions, and this led to his eventual breakup with Kim. However, having already had success in using a woman before, his physical passions trumped his intellect and will, and random make-out sessions with girls he barely knew soon followed.

Andrew recalled, "I settled for what I knew was easy instead of fighting for a girl's heart, which seemed too hard. I got what I wanted without having to respect or date her, but it left me thinking, 'This is it? That was too easy. This can't be what we were meant for.'"

After being introduced to Pope St. John Paul II's Theology of the Body, Andrew finally began to recognize why he desired more from his relationships with women. With this understanding came a longing to uphold the dignity of women in the future. However, he began to wonder if he had what it takes.

"I want to rise to the challenge, but it's scary because I've screwed up in the past, and I don't know if I can do it, even though I want to. The fear is, I've used girls in the past and it worked, and maybe that's all I'll ever be able to do. I now know we're called to a higher love, to respect and court a woman, but I'm afraid I'm not capable of that. There's always this question of, 'Can I measure up?'" Andrew explained.

Fear

Because of the mistakes Rachel and Andrew made in the past, it's understandable why they might allow fear to prevent them from being free to love and be loved. For Rachel, the fear is that she's not good enough or worthy *to be loved*. For Andrew, the fear is that he's inadequate and doesn't have what it takes *to love*.

These are normal fears that perhaps have led you to worry about your future. We get it. Your past has shaped who you are today; however, it does not need to define who you will be for the rest of your life.

Yes, you committed those sins and did those things that you'd rather lock away in the box of shame. But you can't—so we need you to remember that Jesus died for those sins. He died for what you did after that dance. He died for the way you used that person even when you knew something wasn't right. He died for the way you gave in to your selfish desires on that lonely Friday night. He died for the millions of ways in which you have failed to love.

You have sinned and are in need of a savior. Own it, but don't forget that Jesus died for your sins and you were forgiven for them when you took them to Confession. Now it's time to move on with confidence. It's time to no longer allow fear to control you, which is where we will pick up tomorrow.

Today's Detox Challenge

Kathryn shared with us that memories from her past had begun waking her up in the middle of the night. These episodes had plagued her until she decided to do something about them. Before she went to bed, she would wrap a rosary around her hand, bless herself with holy water, and put a St. Benedict's crucifix on her nightstand. If she had any problems, she'd immediately reach for them to help her calm down. The episodes slowly went away.

The quiet hours of the night are one of the easiest times to allow fear to gnaw at us. To help keep the fears at bay, we suggest you do what Kathryn did—gather some of your favorite sacramentals and place them by your bedside. Items can include a Bible opened to a powerful verse, a rosary, holy water, St. Benedict's crucifix, prayer cards, or a statue or image of a favorite saint. Sleep with a scapular, rosary, or holy medals on you. Surround yourself with these powerful spiritual weapons to keep a peaceful disposition, even when you are sleeping.

Day 39: Hope

Yesterday we brought up two fears that could easily prevent you from being free to love and be loved. Whether you realize it or not, much of this book has been focused on helping you conquer those fears, so today let's face them and see why you have every reason to hope.

Fear #1: You Can't Be Loved

Yesterday we heard the story of Rachel, who feared that because of her past mistakes and sins, there was no way somebody could one day truly love her. She worried that she had gone too far and crossed too many lines to be seen as worthy of authentic love. Why would anyone want to pursue and take risks for a girl like her? After all she had done, how could she be loved?

If you've ever asked yourself that question, take hope. Take hope and think back to all the ways throughout this journey that you have come to discover that you are the kind of person who can be loved:

- You've learned that you are an immortal member of a royal family whose Father is the King of Heaven and Earth.

- You've been invited to experience the mercy and forgiveness of your Heavenly Father in Confession, so you can confidently move forward and be merciful and forgiving toward yourself and others.

- You've begun to strive for a real relationship with God through prayer, so you can learn to trust in your Father who loves.

- You've read dozens of stories that prove that it's never too late to start over and be loved, no matter how far you've gone.

- You've learned not to be afraid to heal and move on so that the things that have been done to you do not plague you.

- You've learned to recognize that the moments in which you feel empty are times when God is drawing you closer to him so you can know in a deeper way just how loved you are.

- You've discovered that the God of the universe wants you, and your worth comes from him. You don't need someone else to save you, because you already have a Savior.

All this knowledge has been presented to you to help you know that you are lovable. You can be loved, and you deserve to be loved, because you were made to be loved.

Fear #2: You Don't Have What It Takes to Love

As Andrew shared yesterday, after having used women even when he could feel that it was wrong, he worried that maybe he didn't have what it takes to love properly.

Alfred, who experienced the same fear, put it this way: "It can feel like I'm too inadequate to love. I think, 'That girl's so great, she deserves more than me. I'm so messed up—what if I fall back into using girls?'" Alfred felt the weight of the responsibility he had to uphold the dignity of the women in his life. He desperately wanted to rise to the occasion, but having messed up in the past, the gnawing question was, "Can I do it?"

If you've ever asked yourself that question, take hope. Take hope because throughout this journey you have worked hard to be the kind of person who does have what it takes.

Think about it. This whole process aimed to give you the habits and skills needed to live the virtue of chastity and to love rightly. Here is what you have accomplished over the past thirty-nine days:

- You've worked to identify your triggers, set boundaries for them, and come up with plans for how to deal with them.

- You've begun to lean on virtuous friends and people who will hold you accountable for your goals.

- You've learned about your intellect, will, and passions, and now know that you can control yourself through the practice of virtue.

- You've discovered that you can properly direct your physical and emotional passions in ways that will help you choose love over use.

- You've seen what authentic love looks like by understanding how it is reflected in the love of the Trinity.

- You've realized the difference between physical acts that are meant to arouse and acts that show authentic affection.

- You've made sacrifices to get rid of the bad habits and influences in your life that have prevented you in the past from being able to love.

Do you see it? All these things have been put in motion so you can have what it takes to love properly. Take hope and do not be afraid. You have put in the work; now believe in the power of God moving in you to carry it out. You can do it. You were made to do it because you were made to love.

Today's Detox Challenge

The freedom to love and be loved is staring you in the face. You've struggled and worked hard to get to where you are. Now with confidence we invite you to make a commitment to strive to live out what you have learned on this journey. Below is a pledge that we hope you'll read and take to heart. If you are ready, say a quick prayer and sign it.

The Pledge

I, _____, promise to choose love over use as I strive to live the virtue of chastity so I can be free to love and be loved. I promise to will the good of others and to treat them as people with immortal souls, not things. I will refuse to use people to fill physical or emotional voids. I will let Jesus be my Savior, and even if I don't feel his presence, I will trust that he is there. When I fall, I will get back up again, believing in the mercy of my Heavenly Father. I will not allow the darker moments of my past to define me as I work to heal. I will choose to hope, knowing that God has a plan for my life and created me to be with him forever in Heaven.

Signature _____   Date_____

Day 40: Celebrate

When you picked up this book did you ever doubt whether you'd find yourself here, standing at the summit of your forty-day journey? Well, you did it. You stepped out in faith and began moving toward something that may have seemed impossible to navigate. You tested limits, faced fears, worked to remove toxins, created healthy habits, and persevered to the end. Even if you didn't do everything perfectly, you finished, and that is something you should be deeply proud of. We pray the view from up here is as amazing as you had hoped it would be.

As you soak in your final destination, take the time to reflect on all that you have learned about love, dating, and sex, as well as about yourself, others, and God. Remember the struggles, remember the victories, and thank him for it all.

Even though your forty days of detoxing are complete, the journey of growing in your understanding of authentic love will continue. We have tried to cover as many needs as we could, but surely there are issues that we have missed. Each person who picks up this book is so unique that it would be impossible for us to create a guide that addresses every potential need of every potential reader. There will always be more summits to scale, so from here it's up to you to seek out your next fourteener.

Keep Climbing

If you are willing to challenge yourself to continually strive for holiness, there will always be new ways to grow in virtue. Keep climbing. Keep testing your limits. Keep facing your fears. Keep struggling to fight the good fight. When you fall down, get back up again. When you want to quit, look to Heaven and let Jesus be your strength. When you feel as though you are never going to get there, remember this: your final destination isn't on this earth anyway.

You have an immortal soul that was made for Heaven, and as long as you are here on earth, it will continue to long for Heaven. Let that thought carry you when all else fails. Your reward awaits you in Heaven, and when you get to paradise it will all have been worth it.

Stories

Perhaps your favorite part of this book was the stories threaded throughout it. Reading the accounts of the many interviewees who bravely shared their process of moving from "I want this" to "I'm living it" probably struck a chord with you. Perhaps you often found yourself able to relate to their feelings and experiences, and perhaps their stories left you reflecting on your own life. We hope they encouraged you to persevere in trusting that if they could do it, then so can you. We hope their stories changed your life.

Today as you finish this book, you now have your own story to tell, a story that is uniquely yours and yet universally relatable. It's a story that, if shared, will strike a chord with others who are longing to move from "I want this" to "I'm living it." You, too, have a story that can change lives.

Remember those friends we talked about on Day 29? The ones we didn't want you to shun? The ones we wanted you to pray for that you might have the opportunity to walk with them on their own journey? Well, we want you to share your story with one of those friends.

Who is it that needs to experience the freedom that comes from living a life that is focused on love and not use? Do you know anyone who needs to be told, "You are an immortal member of a royal family with a worth and dignity that is too great to settle for being used as a thing"? Love these people enough to challenge them to something greater. Tell them your story.

We are honored that you have trusted us to guide you on this path. From the depths of our hearts, thank you. We are praying for you, now and always.

Be saints—it's worth it!

Today's Detox Challenge

We do not want you to keep this book. We want you to give it away to that someone you know who needs it. "But I already signed my name after the pledge!" you say? No problem—they can just sign their name below yours. Besides, can you imagine how amazing it would be to receive this book with multiple signatures in it and know that you are not the first, or the last, to walk this journey?

Who needs to hear your story? We hope you will send a text right now and tell that person you want to talk. Your story just might change a life.

Discussion Questions for Week 6

1. Throughout the book, there has been an emphasis on the need for Jesus to help you rather than you trying to do everything on your own. What are some ways that you have needed Jesus in your life this week?

2. There are a lot of fears when it comes to living a life of authentic love: fears about whether you can be healed of past scars, fears about whether or not someone can be loved again, fears about finding a spouse. How have these forty days of detoxing helped you in a practical way to face these fears and build habits to overcome them?

3. What's the most difficult challenge you faced during this detox?

4. What's your one key takeaway from this book?

5. Moving forward, what are you hoping to continue to work on?

6. Are you planning to share your story with anyone? How do you plan to do this?

Endnotes

Foreword

[1] Carolyn Bradshaw, Arnold S. Kahn, and Bryan K. Saville, "To Hook Up or Date: Which Gender Benefits?" *Sex Roles* 62 (2010): 661–669.

[2] Elizabeth L. Paul and Kristen A. Hayes, "The Casualties of 'Casual' Sex: A Qualitative Exploration of the Phenomenology of College Students' Hook-ups," *Journal of Social and Personal Relationships* 19 (2002): 639–661.

[3] Justin R. Garcia et al., "Touch Me in the Morning: Intimately Affiliative Gestures in Uncommitted and Romantic Relationships" (paper presented at the Annual Conference of the Northeastern Evolutionary Psychology Society, New Paltz, NY, March 2010).

[4] Nancy Jo Sales, "Tinder and the Dawn of the 'Dating Apocalypse,'" *Vanity Fair*, August 6, 2015.

Week 1

[1] If you need a starting point, check out *In Conversation with God* by Francis Fernandez or *The Imitation of Christ* by Thomas à Kempis.

Week 2

[1] C. S. Lewis, *The Weight of Glory* (New York: HarperOne, 2001), 46.

[2] Karol Wojtyla, *Love and Responsibility*, trans. H. T. Willetts (San Francisco: Ignatius Press, 1993), 42.

[3] There are also theological virtues, but for simplicity's sake we are only going to address the moral, or human, virtues in this book.

Week 3

[1] For more about this topic, see CCC 1601–66.

[2] Liqun Han, Liwei Wang, Stephani C. Wang, and Hai-Peng Yang, "Nonsocial Functions of Hypothalamic Oxytocin," *ISRN Neuroscience* (2013), doi: 10.1155/2013/179272.

[3] If you're still wrestling with this issue we suggest you listen to Janet Smith's *Contraception: Cracking the Myths* audio CD, which is available through the Augustine Institute.

[4] *The Collected Letters of C. S. Lewis,* ed. Walter Hooper, vol. 3, *1950-1963* (New York: HarperOne, 2007), 758.

Week 4

1   For more on this topic see *Love and Responsibility* by Karol Wojtyla, now Pope St. John Paul II, 73–82, 101–18.

2   Wojtyla, *Love and Responsibility*, 112.

3   Wojtyla, *Love and Responsibility*, 78.

Week 5

1   Carolyn Dawn Johnson, "One Day Closer to You", written by Carolyn Dawn Johnson and Mary Danna, produced by Paul Worley and Carolyn Dawn Johnson, on *Room With a View*. Arista Nashville/BMG 07863-69336-2, 2001, compact disc.